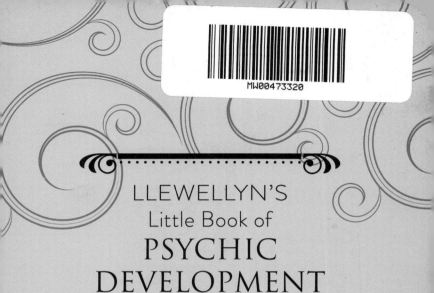

LLEWELLYN'S
Little Book of
PSYCHIC
DEVELOPMENT

MELANIE BARNUM

LLEWELLYN PUBLICATIONS
WOODBURY, MINNESOTA

FIRST EDITION
Third Printing, 2020

Book design by Rebecca Zins
Book format by Bob Gaul
Cover cartouche by Freepik
Cover design by Lisa Novak
Editing by Aaron Lawrence

Llewellyn Publications is a registered trademark of Llewellyn Worldwide Ltd.

Library of Congress Cataloging-in-Publication Data
Names: Barnum, Melanie, author.
Title: Llewellyn's little book of psychic development.
Other titles: Little book of psychic development
Description: Woodbury: Llewellyn Worldwide, Ltd, 2017. | Includes
 bibliographical references.
Identifiers: LCCN 2017000160 (print) | LCCN 2017005291 (ebook) | ISBN
 9780738751863 | ISBN 9780738752600 (ebook)
Subjects: LCSH: Parapsychology. | Psychic ability. |
Intuition—Miscellanea.
Classification: LCC BF1031 .B258 2017 (print) | LCC BF1031 (ebook) | DDC
 131.8—dc23
LC record available at https://lccn.loc.gov/2017000160

Llewellyn Worldwide Ltd. does not participate in, endorse, or have any authority or responsibility concerning private business transactions between our authors and the public.

All mail addressed to the author is forwarded, but the publisher cannot, unless specifically instructed by the author, give out an address or phone number.

Any Internet references contained in this work are current at publication time, but the publisher cannot guarantee that a specific location will continue to be maintained. Please refer to the publisher's website for links to authors' websites and other sources.

NOTE: The information in this book is not meant to diagnose, treat, prescribe, or substitute consultation with a licensed healthcare professional.

Llewellyn Publications
A Division of Llewellyn Worldwide Ltd.
2143 Wooddale Drive
Woodbury, MN 55125-2989
www.llewellyn.com

Printed in China

My family not only puts up with my crazy writing schedule, they encourage it. For that, and so much more, I thank you Tom, Molly, and Samantha!

Without your unconditional love, none of this would be worth it!

Contents

૭જી

Exercises

INTRODUCTION
*Why Me, Why You,
Why This Book?*

Most people would not look at me and consider me to be a New Ager or a Spiritualist, not that there would be anything wrong with that. I don't pretend to know everything or to know what you are thinking at any given point in time. I don't walk around in flowing robes, a multicolored scarf wrapped around my head. Well, maybe I do wear scarfs, and usually I wear big hoop earrings, but that doesn't mean I fit the rest of the stereotypical traits of being a fortune-teller. I am a mother and wife, a sister, and a friend. I am an average woman. I am quite comfortable living in my house with my beautiful daughters and my wonderful husband; I prefer to have a home base rather than a traveling caravan moving from one location to the next, as typically associated with Gypsies. I do, however, believe that if that is who you are, then by all means go for it. I too have gone for it. You see, I *am* a professional psychic and a medium.

This means that the people in my town who don't know me, and even those who do, may look at me a bit differently than they would any other typical woman. I know they sometimes wonder if I'm crazy or just plain ridiculous. These, I believe, are the ones who just don't recognize yet how powerful and incredible intuition and psychic abilities can be. They don't know that you can tune in to help yourself and others. And, even more importantly, they don't realize they *already* tune in!

Luckily for me, that doesn't matter. I *do* know how amazing it is to be able to use my psychic gifts to assist others with their everyday life and even their most important life questions. I work with clients—in my office in Ridgefield, Connecticut, and on the phone—who want answers regarding their past, their present, and their future. Sometimes they are also hoping to connect with their deceased loved ones. This is what I do, and this is how I know I am *not* crazy or ridiculous—I am just psychic.

Getting to Know Me

My work is not limited to clients. It also includes, of course, my family and friends as well. Take Grace, for instance. Grace is a good friend, practically a sister, who was looking to perhaps purchase a beach house in Rhode Island. She texted me while I was in the middle of getting ready to head out for a day filled with college cheer competitions for my oldest daughter. I was busy running around and definitely not thinking about tapping into my abilities. I usually try to shut that part of me down a bit so I can focus on other things when I'm not working, but that doesn't always happen.

Grace asked me which house she should focus on, if any. She wanted me to help her cut out the stress of whittling down the various properties. If I could make her decision easier, she was all for it. So, I tuned in briefly as I was drying my hair. Again, I was in a hurry and had a long day ahead. What I saw confused me. I got, in my mind's eye, an image of a smallish, weathered brown house that needed some TLC. But that wasn't what confused me. What made me second-guess myself was that I also saw a gray and white building. I wasn't sure what that meant but decided to tell her anyway. It would be on a dirt road and have a sand or gravel driveway. I also felt she was on the water but saw conflicting symbolic information. I had a flash of bicycles, which, if you've ever rented a place in Rhode Island or any other shore town, you'd know represents the common mode of transportation that takes you to the beach when you are block or two away.

I texted her everything I received, although I wasn't sure exactly what it meant. After all, I hadn't physically seen any of the properties she was considering and didn't know why I was getting inconsistent information. The brown I was seeing was definitely different from the gray and white colors I saw. I also told her I saw a bunch of orangey balls, the letter *C* was standing out, and I was getting a reference to "beans." She immediately wrote me back and told me she knew exactly which property I meant, and she would be putting an offer on it that day!

I thought to myself, *Wow ... that's a lot of pressure. She is putting an offer in on a house despite the fact that I'm giving her conflicting colors and information. I hope she knows what she's doing and is choosing the right one.*

The next day she sent me a picture with a note that said she had indeed put an offer on the house I saw in my vision. The image showed a weathered brown house, and immediately next to it was a large gray shed with white trim. The property bordered a pond, and the Rhode Island beach was down the road, accessible by bicycles. She couldn't think of any significant C words and had no idea what the bean reference was about. I joked and told her maybe she just needed more fiber in her diet! We continued laughing as we discussed the lack of orangey balls on the property. Overall, though, it sounded like what I had seen clairvoyantly with my psychic sight (see chapter 3: Understanding Your Basic Psychic Gifts).

This is my life; whether I am driving my girls around or going out with my husband and my wonderful friends, I am always psychic. It can be turned down and put on the back burner, but it never fully goes away. I have always been able to read people. I didn't know way back then, however, that everyone else didn't do this, too. Professionally, it all began for me about two decades ago, seemingly out of the blue.

Intuition was a generally accepted part of our lives, even if we didn't recognize it for what it was. Growing up in a single mother household meant we always had to trust in our gut instincts. Though we were lucky to have a roof over our heads and hand-me-down clothes, survival was usually the focus of my mom, and by the trickle-down theory, it spread to all of us. I think we all "read" people in our own way. My sister, always intuitive, used to see people as colors. Later I understood that to be their aura (see chapter 2: Energy, Meditation, and Symbols). My brother never really discussed it, but you could tell if he did or did not get a good vibe off of someone almost instantly. And then there was me. I just thought feeling someone's energy was a common part of life—that there was nothing special about it.

I didn't grow up homeless, and I was not abused. I was never in a coma and I did not have a near-death experience. This is how I know that normal everyday people like myself can access their own personal sixth sense. I discovered my gifts after I was metaphysically hit over the head and I heard the words, "You need to do this work now." I looked for the source of the voice. At that time, I didn't regularly or even occasionally hear voices telling me what to do. But on this day, I did. There was no one there, not even my husband. It was what I believe to be my guides from the other side letting me know that it was time I took it to the next level.

My first instinct was, "*No way!*" But, after much inner debate and denial, although I felt it was an impossibility that I was going to begin advertising as a professional psychic, the likelihood of *not* following the directive was nonexistent. I needed to heed the advice of my newly discovered spiritual friends and start doing the work. So, that is exactly what I set out to do. I took classes to legitimize what I was discovering to be a natural talent, and I studied with world-famous teachers as well as local ones until I felt comfortable offering free psychic readings. This built up my confidence to the point where I realized I was ready to actually hang that shingle and start my career as a professional psychic medium.

My calling, so far, has been to help others through my readings and my healing work. I pursued accreditations in many modalities. I studied just about everything, from hypnotherapy to reflexology to past-life regression to Reiki to psychic detective certifications. And I don't ever want to stop learning. I also very much enjoy teaching others to tune in. This allows me to help other people discover their own aptitudes while I continue my pursuit of knowledge by training others. The universe is vast, and I truly believe there is so much more for me to accomplish! My life, like yours, is ever evolving.

Getting to Know You

Who are you? Why would you want to develop your psychic abilities? What could they do for you? Imagine living a life filled with positivity and abundance. Can you visualize what that would be like? Many can't. There may be a few simple reasons for that. Possibly you believe nothing comes easy, that nothing comes without a lot of hard, backbreaking work. Or maybe you don't feel as though you deserve to have everything you want, or if not everything, at least some semblance of happiness. But deep down inside you *do* know, don't you? You feel that this lifetime is meant to be enjoyed and lived to the fullest. In order to do that, you need to tune in; you need to believe that you can be and do anything you want. And, in order for that to happen, you have to tap into who you are. Are you ready?

I will assume since you are still reading that you *are* ready. This is good. It is your turn to begin channeling your messages, or if you've already started, it's time to increase that flow. You may be feeling as though you are on the edge of a precipice, about to jump in, but feel rooted to the place you currently are by fear. Fully committing to anything is difficult, but magnifying that by the fact that psychic abilities can be mysterious, at the very least, can create an intimidating sensation. Knowing that you are prepared to continue learning helps you take that first step into this way of life. Imagine all that is available for you to tap into—gifts that were previously viewed as something only mystics could enjoy. It's your time.

Many of us have a tendency to put others first. Often, it becomes the norm. This doesn't mean that you won't ever put yourself first. We all do from time to time. But when we are looking to create time to do something for us, something that could change the world for us, we are very adept at coming up with excuses:

- I have to take care of my kids before I can do anything for me.
- When my children move out, then I will have time for me.
- My husband needs me right now.
- I am the sole supporter for my family; I can't jeopardize that by taking time off.
- There are other things more important than learning to use my intuition.
- My wife thinks psychic stuff is crazy.
- I don't believe I could ever be as good as Johnny.

But what do you think would happen if you just changed these thoughts around a bit? How about allowing for the possibility that maybe, just maybe, you *are* worth the time and energy to dive into what could be a total game changer for you and your family.

- I am taking care of my kids by taking care of me.
- I want my children to enjoy everything they can before they move out.
- My husband needs the best me I can be.
- I am the sole supporter for my family; I can't jeopardize that by not increasing my psychic abilities.
- There are no other things more important right now than learning to use my intuition.
- My wife thinks psychic stuff is crazy because she hasn't learned about it yet.
- I don't know whether I could ever be as good as Johnny, but I'd love to try.

By changing your viewpoint, you are opening up to endless possibilities to engage in your intuitive birthright. And, yes, it is a birthright. It is something we are born with, regardless of nationality, race, or creed, and it is something we can learn to utilize. Once we become aware of the probability that we possess this legacy, no matter who we are, we can set out to recognize it. Perhaps you have already started your learning process or are intrigued by others who have. This is awesome, and it should tell you that you are ready to revive what may already be a somewhat dormant part of your life.

At the very least you should be aware of the fun that is ahead of you and waiting for you to jump into what will most likely be an incredible experience. Don't let the challenge of all that awaits you hold you back any longer. You possess the muscles to transform your life, to manifest an abundance of powerful intuitive gifts. Remember, you picked right now to make changes; your toes are gripping the edge of the precipice of amazement. Falling backward will only stall the inevitable positivity available for you. If you live with one foot in the past, you will never live in the present or be able to fully extend toward your future. Jump in!

Loving This Book!

We've all gotten books we were excited about, only to be let down because they did not provide what they promised. This will not be one of those. You've picked this book, which tells you that you are on your way to developing your psychic abilities. This is so exciting! But the question still remains—what will you get out of the book? What can it do for you? You will get out of it what you put into it. In it there are true stories, explanations, and hands-on exercises to help you in virtually every aspect of your life. How would you like to:

- Feel more connected to your spirit?
- Feel more connected to the universe?
- Improve and enhance your current, future, and even past relationships?
- Receive help when making decisions in every area of your life?
- Have the perfect career?
- Increase your creativity?
- Connect to your loved ones and guides on the other side?
- Love yourself?

If you answered yes to any of these, you have picked the right book!

Throughout these pages you will have the opportunity to practice tuning in to your intuition. The exercises within will be an integral and important component in developing your psychic abilities. You will be introduced to some new concepts and probably be reacquainted with some that are more familiar. You can expect to be transported at times to places you can only see in your mind's eye. Look forward to hearing answers to your questions that no one else hears and get ready to know things that you can't possibly know.

If this is the first time you've explored your psychic abilities, you probably won't finish this book and feel like you can go out and charge money for professional readings with any semblance of accuracy. But you will learn to respect the gifts you have and acknowledge how much more there is out there to fully comprehend. You can definitely expect to walk away with a deep-seated wisdom that can also give you greater advantages in many areas of your life, including your career and relationships. You may experience a psychic hit, the validation that something you receive psychically was correct. One thing is for certain; you will be assured that you have more natural talent than you have ever given yourself credit for.

Look at it from a different perspective. There is currently a trend to try to understand how intuition and psychic awareness works. We want to figure out how others do it so we can begin to emulate their styles. Take the more famous ones, for instance. There are many psychic mediums on television that bring it more into the public eye. In my humble opinion, there are many incredibly funny, compassionate, and real psychics on TV. For the most part, they are very good at what they do. However, if you try to repeat how successful they are on TV, you will surely be let down. This is because as tremendously accurate as they may be, they are never 100 percent. We see the edited version: the good, meaty stuff. Like any other talented professional medium, they are not always right. We see them on the shows interpreting information and messages in their own way, and we catch mere minutes of readings, not the remaining hour or so. Give yourself a little leeway. While you're learning, and even if you decide to practice on others or professionally, you will not always be without error. In addition, the person you are reading for will not always recognize the messages you are bringing to them.

Practicing and actually tuning in is such an important part of learning to use your gifts; a journal and a pen will come in handy for many of the upcoming exercises. This journal is yours to keep for reference later on and also to review how much you've accomplished. Beyond that, an open mind and a willingness to learn are all you need to succeed in developing your psychic abilities!

• EXERCISE 1 •
Your Goals

Get out that journal and pen now. Open to the first page and write "Psychic Journal" in the middle in giant letters to set your intention. Turn to the next page and write "Psychic Goals" on the top. Then, make a list of what you'd like to learn, beginning with the first thing that pops into your mind. Include even the largest of your own psychic development goals, even if they seem improbable. Do not discount anything as being too grand, such as learning how to do public readings at big events for celebrities, or even too small, like intuiting how to psychically know who is calling when your phone rings. What you want to get out of this book is important. Remember, psychic abilities develop differently for everyone, and who is to say you won't be the next great psychic!

TIPS

- You possess the means to develop your abilities right now!

- You need to practice and tune in to learn to use your gifts!

Chapter One

WHAT IS PSYCHIC DEVELOPMENT?

Psychic development means to practice, in some way, and increase your knowledge of psychic abilities. It is with curiosity that most people make the conscious or sometimes unconscious decision to jump in, maybe only one toe at a time, to learn what they can or cannot do psychically.

Are You Born with It?

People are born with a natural gift that allows them to tune in to their intuition. Some are more adept at this. Because our gifts are subtle, we don't always recognize that we are using them or even that we have them. If you're reading this right now, you have to know you've definitely got something going on—you've already begun your journey. But, just like any other ability or talent, not everyone will be at the same level of expertise as others.

This does not mean that you are unable to increase these gifts, however. Simple things like meditation and training will help propel you to the next stage of your development. Practice will not necessarily make perfect, but it will increase your abilities as your knowledge grows. Expanding your fundamental awareness of everything psychic will create a deeper understanding as well. Don't get frustrated. Your gifts are there, just waiting to be explored and developed.

Psychic abilities are often more pronounced in people who have had difficulties during childhood or during their adolescent years. People who strive to fit in or struggle with their identities may also find they have a more in-tune sense. Those who've had to be on constant high alert due to abuse or even geographical location may also find their natural intuition has helped them to survive. Someone who is constantly concerned for their safety or the safety of others they care about will often discover that their instincts will assist them in protecting those they love. All of these things can, but don't always, lead to heightened intuitive senses.

There are numerous other ways in which our natural intuition may be jump started without putting forth any effort to make it happen. Many people develop their psychic abilities after a life-altering event, such as losing a parent or a sibling. Another trigger can be having a near-death experience. For example, surviving a severe car accident or being struck by lightning and waking to discover you died for a few seconds but have been revived can give you a deeper awareness and talent to access your psychic gifts.

All of the above circumstances can lead to a deeper level of intuitive abilities, but they are not necessary to naturally connect. My story, thankfully, had none of the pain or trauma connected to the difficulties described above. I just believed there was more to life than what we could conceivably imagine; well, that and I felt like someone hit me over the head! The mere acknowledgment that the possibility is there to tap in to the vast wisdom of the universe can often be enough to embark on a metaphysical journey of psychic development.

• EXERCISE 2 •
When You First Discover It

Open your journal to a new page, with pen in hand. Now, close your eyes and take a deep breath through your nose. Pay attention to how your breath flows in and travels down through your chest, into your lungs. Notice how it feels as you exhale through your mouth. Take a few more deep breaths.

When you find you are relaxed, allow your mind to travel back in time. Continue all the way back to the first moment you remember experiencing intuition in any way. Once you've retrieved that first memory, try to go back even earlier. When you feel you've recalled as far back as you can, open your eyes and put your pen to your paper to answer these questions:

- Where were you?
- How old were you?
- Were you alone or with others?
- How did it feel?
- Did you share what happened with anyone?

- Did you recognize it as intuition or a psychic episode right away?

- Did it scare you?

- Did it comfort you?

- Did it occur after any kind of traumatic event or troubling situation?

- Finally, what was it?

If you remember back even further after you finish this exercise, go ahead and answer the same questions again. Notice if they feel different in any way or if you answer them differently than you did the first time.

What Are Psychic Abilities?

I am asked all the time, "What does it mean to be psychic?" One may think this is an easy question to answer, but being psychic can mean many different things. In its purest essence, being psychic means being able to connect to and extract or receive information that pertains to someone's past, present, or future that would not otherwise be accessible in our physical plane. It implies using senses other than our normal five corporeal senses. In general, psychic ability means being aware of things that you have no reason to be conscious of or knowing things without possessing evidence of where or how you've come to know them—you just know them. It also means you are able to interpret the messages you are receiving. It is this interaction, even if it only feels one-sided, that often separates your five physical senses from a psychic hit.

Possessing psychic abilities also means that you have a metaphysical intelligence. You are gifted with the power to be a conduit to another dimension. You are communicating with a presence that others probably don't acknowledge, and you are able to interpret the knowledge you are receiving. It is this interaction, even if it only feels one-sided, that often separates your five psychical senses from a psychic hit.

Are Psychic Abilities the Same As Intuition?

There is often confusion about what qualifies as psychic gifts and intuition. Psychic abilities are kind of the next step above intuition and, in fact, many people use the words interchangeably. Though it can feel somewhat ambiguous, the best way to describe the difference is that while everyone is naturally intuitive, not everyone will be a natural psychic. You can compare this to the fact that while everyone can splash some paint onto a canvas, not everyone will be as gifted as Leonardo da Vinci. Whether it's a mother's intuition, a gut instinct, or just a strong sense about something personal, for most of us intuition plays a role in our daily lives. Some, however, can bring that intuition to the next level.

Let's use an extreme example to show the difference between intuition and psychic ability. Pretend there was a body found and the police did not know whether the person died from natural causes or was murdered. If they were to ask you and you had a bad feeling, or you felt like something was wrong, that may just be your basic gut instinct. But, if you were to feel the actual cause of death and possibly see in your mind's eye how the person died or even who killed them, those would all be indicative of psychic awareness. Feeling that something is off can also be a psychic ability if it is very strong. Psychic hits tend to be more pronounced and perceived with more detail than intuition.

There is no distinct line between intuition and psychic gifts. Being intuitive does not negate being psychic, and vice versa. Psychic abilities can be developed and learned, yet everyone will excel to different levels. Even practicing psychics, those like me who offer professional readings, may not connect at the same level as their peers. Everyone has their own link and interpretation. When you develop your abilities, you will generally go as far as you want depending upon how much you put into it. Psychic abilities can be tricky to grasp sometimes, and plentiful (see chapter 3: Understanding Your Basic Psychic Gifts). Just because you know what they are and what you want to do with them doesn't mean you will become adept with the specific one you want. Practicing with extrasensory perception will help you develop your various psychic gifts and also bring forth the ones you are more proficient with.

• EXERCISE 3 •
Your Abilities

Turn to a fresh page and write down your ideas on psychic abilities. Include your hopes and desires around the development of your own gifts as well as any fears you may have surrounding psychic abilities. Do you feel you have a steady connection to your abilities, or are you trying to create the connection? Look at what you've written down. Do your answers surprise you?

If I Turn It On, Can I Turn It Off?

The Internet and television tend to portray psychics as all-knowing and never stopping. They are shown to be constantly tuned in and continually active, and while a few are always open to receiving messages, most are not. Being a professional doesn't mean you are always working. Imagine what would happen if you continuously had someone else's stuff rolling through your mind. You'd never be able to focus on the here and now, or even on your own daily life. We are able to turn it off. Even though we are in contact with the other side, we are able to turn it down, like turning down a radio. We can listen to the music if we want or we can choose to turn it all the way down so it doesn't distract or bother us. We are also able to change the station if we don't like what's playing, just like we can disconnect with energy if we no longer want to communicate with it.

For some of us, this can be a more difficult task. If you've fallen into your gifts without trying, compartmentalizing and choosing when you will use them may be something you need to learn to control. For example, yesterday I watched the movie *The Sixth Sense* with my daughter Samantha. She is all too aware of the realities that the actor Haley Joel Osment faced in the movie when he had a continuous parade of dead people showing up in his room. For him, it just happened. He didn't ask for it, nor did he try to develop it. It just scared him until he learned to maintain some semblance of control over it. Samantha, too, used to wake up to a barrage of spirits in her room on a regular basis. This continued for quite a while, no matter how often I cleared the room's energy with sage and intention. The interruptions continued until she learned to control it and turn it off.

For me personally, it sometimes feels as though I am walking through quicksand if I am unintentionally staying in my psychic place. I get a kind of spacey feeling. Most of us won't ever have to worry about not being able to shut down our intuition in order to function in our daily lives. More often than not, the feeling of heaviness will not affect you, but it's always good to know how to tame it so it doesn't interfere with the rest of your life.

Whether you have a hard time shutting down your intuition or you simply want to know how to protect yourself from any negativity, "exercise 4" will be one of the most important for you to keep in your bag of psychic knowledge. Whenever you need to protect yourself—and before attempting any type of psychic connection—it is important to perform this meditation.

• EXERCISE 4 •
Control the Flow

Go to a place where you can relax without being disturbed. You will need at least ten minutes of peace and quiet to truly allow this exercise to work for you. You can also separate the first part from the second and use them in different situations as the need arises.

Begin by closing your eyes and breathing deeply, paying attention to how the breath feels as you inhale slowly and exhale even slower. Continue focusing on your breath and begin to feel your body slowing down, relaxing even further. Good.

Now, reach your left hand out in front of you, palm up. With your eyes still closed, hold your right hand up in front of your mouth in a tunnel shape and blow through it; imagine you are blowing bubbles. Allow the largest bubble to land on your left hand and let your right hand gently fall back down to your side. Feel the bubble expanding, getting bigger and bigger. As it continues to grow, allow it to encompass your hand and begin to spread around your arm, growing even larger. As your arm moves down to your side, feel the bubble moving to surround your body, from the bottoms of your feet to the top of your head.

Your bubble of protection allows only positive energy to enter, and actually repels negativity. Imagine your bubble is glowing a beautiful silvery white sparkly color that pulses with your energy as you watch it. Allow this bubble to expand even further, bringing into it your family and your home, keeping them safe and protected.

Next, with your bubble still surrounding you and your eyes still closed, focus your attention on the top of your head, your crown chakra area (see chapter 2: Energy, Meditation, and Symbols). Imagine a sparkly, shiny water faucet above your body that you can turn on and off. Water can help carry psychic energy. This faucet, floating at the top of your head just above your bubble, can control the flow with which the psychic messages come through.

It is your choice how open your psychic faucet is. You can regulate it at all times. Imagine reaching your hand up and turning the handle so the flow is wide open. Allow yourself to receive the message energy rushing into your bubble, the warmth fluidly bathing your body, mind, and spirit. Feel your crown chakra adjusting and spinning like a wheel as it takes it all in. Bask in the positive energy of the universe for a moment.

Now, turn the handle off gradually, letting the steady flow turn to a soft drip. Notice how it feels as the energy that is coming into your bubble slows down. Pay attention specifically to how your head feels; you may experience a tingly sensation, or it may possibly feel as though your head becomes lighter. Allow the energy to continue, without burden or weight, as a very thin, relaxed trickle. Leaving it slightly open like this provides you with the opportunity to tap in to it at will. If you feel overwhelmed at all at any time, close it completely. You can always adjust the flow when necessary.

You now have the power to regulate the current of psychic information. You can turn it on or off like a water fountain, simply by opening or closing the faucet. Take advantage of it! When you need to tune in, the information will be there, waiting for you to access it.

Are You Afraid?

Religion and learned or even ingrained beliefs can cause you to develop an unhealthy view of psychic abilities. I can't begin to tell you the number of times I've been told that I talk to the devil. I once received a series of phone calls from an older gentleman who had heard me on a paranormal show and decided to take it upon himself to heal and save me from the devil inside me. Even friends sometimes have a hard time not only believing in what I do but understanding that I'm not in cahoots with evil entities. A lot of this is due to ignorance—not meant in a mean way—but because they don't know or they've never experienced any of this for themselves. Many also have a hard time because they believe God is the only one who can connect to higher knowing. Also, it's difficult for some to understand that your own energy or higher self can connect to the energy around you. Practicing or using your psychic gifts does not belittle religion or contradict previously held beliefs about intuition or extrasensory abilities. It doesn't have to be one or the other; it can be both.

The belief that psychic communication is bad can unfortunately deter many people from developing their gifts. It can cause you to feel guilty when you discover you are actually intuitive and even more so when you *want* to develop your psychic abilities! Learning where the information comes from and understanding that you can control the energy you receive helps to lessen the fear that you will be possessed if you give in to the ultimate urge to cultivate your gifts.

Invite Everyone to the Party ... Where Does the Information Really Come From

Life goes on. Of course you've probably heard this before, but this takes it to a whole new dimension, literally. Connecting to the other side is connecting to lives that have passed from the physical plane and moved on to the metaphysical plane. This includes, of course, your loved ones and friends. You can also communicate with your personal spirit guides and angels who have information to share.

This is where your messages are coming from, and they will send these messages to you as often and as clearly as they possibly can. Just ask for it.

We are not alone, ever. We have guides who walk with us, side by side, though we may never become aware that they are there. These are spirits that have our best interests as their agenda, and they can help us develop our psychic abilities. Our spirit guides have walked the earth before. In other words, they have been alive at one time, just like you or me. Generally, however, they will not have been our closest relatives, though they may have been related to us many generations removed. They are responsible for sending us information to help us work through practical dilemmas because they have experienced the same types of trials and tribulations in their human lives. Spirit guides assist us when we ask for specific help. They are a great source to help us solve our personal problems.

We also have our deceased loved ones who, like our guides, have lived. They are there to help us with our daily life and to let us know that they still love us and watch over us. Angels, on the other hand, have never lived. They are the ones who sweep in for the big stuff, the life-altering stuff. They are not your everyday helpers; rather, angels hang around to help us with our major life lessons.

• EXERCISE 5 •
Meet Your Helpers

Find somewhere you will not be disturbed, somewhere you can freely relax. Bring your journal and a pen so you can record information when you are done with the exercise. Sit or lie down comfortably and close your eyes. Begin again by paying attention to your breath. Breathe in and feel the oxygen traveling throughout your body. Breathe out and feel any negative energy dissipate and leave. After you've done this a couple times, you should feel more relaxed. If not, you can continue focusing on your breath and how it feels as you inhale and exhale.

Using the protection part of the meditation from the last exercise, "Control the Flow," begin by encircling yourself with your safety bubble. It's always a good idea to protect yourself before any type of psychic meditation or work. Feel the bubble extending way out, at least twenty feet away from you, keeping you secure inside.

Now imagine yourself at the beginning of a pebble walkway. This walkway is a gently curving path through a beautiful meadow filled with flowers of all shapes and colors. The swaying green grass lulls you into an even deeper meditation as you walk steadily down this path.

You now see a beautiful gazebo in the distance. As you get closer, you count the sides; there are eight in total, with one entrance directly in front of you and one on the opposite side. Move onto the path and sit on the bench to your left, which gives you a direct line of sight down the path you've just come from, as well as the path leading away from the second opening. Take a deep breath.

Notice now that there is someone coming down this new path toward you. This is your spirit guide, one of your helpers. As they make their way into the gazebo, they sit opposite you on another bench. Pay attention to how they look.

- Are they wearing clothing? If so, what does it look like?
- Do they have hair? If so, note the color and style. If not, notice what else may be there.
- Are they tall? Short? Thin or heavy?
- Do they walk? Float?
- Is there any type of glow to them, or are they dull? Are they "normal"?

They want to tell you their name. Allow them to share with you what you can call them from now on. If it's not clear, ask them to repeat it. If it's still difficult to hear them, ask them to spell it out or write in on the floor in the dust.

Now, hold out your hands. They have brought a gift for you. Accept it and thank them for caring for you and helping you every day, in every way. Then look at the gift.

- What is it?
- Is it big? Small?
- Is it a literal or figurative gift?
- Does it mean something special to you?
- Do you understand what it is?
- Did you expect to receive this gift?
- Do you like it?

- Does it bother you or scare you?

- Does it make you sad?

- Does it make you happy?

After you've noticed everything there is about the gift, once again thank your helper.

Now, ask them if there is anything they'd like to tell you and pay attention to what they have to say. It may be one word or even just a sound, or it may be a full sentence or even an entire paragraph. They may show you what they want you to know. Repeat it back to them to help you remember what they've told you or shown you, and again say thank you and allow them to move away from you and back down their path.

After you've taken a few breaths, you can open your eyes. Record everything you've experienced in your journal. Now, with your conscience mind, review what you've written.

Does anything make more sense? Was their visit significant? Did you recognize your guide? Write down all of your thoughts and reread it until you feel comfortable with your experience!

Believe It!

The biggest deterrent to connecting to the other side is—wait for it—YOU! You simply need to believe that you can. You have to allow that there is more to this life than what you can hold or what you can touch. Believe there is a higher energy here to help you. Just like you discovered in the previous exercise, consider there is more to explore and be introduced to.

Be open to your own potential instead of discounting how incredible you are. Understand that you are a significant contributing factor in the universe. Are you excited? You should be. Be enthusiastic about all of the possibilities you are tapping into by connecting to your psychic self.

TIPS

- Notice which word resonates with you more; intuition or psychic?

- You're in control.

- You can always ask for your helpers to send you messages.

- Be open to your vast potential!

TAKE-AWAY

Most of us won't ever have to worry about not being able to shut down our intuition in order to function in our daily lives. More often than not, the feeling of heaviness created by psychic overload will not affect you, but it's always good to know how to tame it so it doesn't interfere with the rest of your life.

Chapter Two

ENERGY, MEDITATION, AND SYMBOLS

Energy plays a major role in developing psychic abilities and your intuitive gifts. Everything is energy. We are, all of us, made of energy, and all energy is connected. Understanding this makes it easier to fathom the possibility that we are able to read energy from people and use our higher self to connect to the energy of others. Often, meditation can assist us in making those energetic connections. Before almost every reading, I sit and do a quick meditation and connect to my own energy by tapping into my etheric energy centers in my body, known as chakras. I ask my guides to connect to the guides and loved ones of my clients to help me access information within their aura, the energy field that emanates from their bodies and connects to their chakras and the energy of the universe. Translating the symbolic information I receive from my client's energy from the other side helps smooth the operation and allows me to comprehend what I am picking up psychically.

Mind, Body, and Spirit Connection

We have an amazing capacity to learn because we are able to process information using every aspect of our being. I am talking about the mind, body, and spirit connection. One cannot properly function without the other, as they are not completely autonomous. Rather, they enhance each other. The mind, being the processing center for perceiving information by analyzing and making judgments, or categorizing data, is able to sort through all types of kinesthetic input and access memories to learn. The body uses its own set of sensory inputs through our physical touch, or nerve sensors, cells, and neurons, which allow us to gain information through our five physical senses: sight, smell, touch, taste, and hearing. And finally, our spirit. Our spirit is what drives us, what keeps us alive and wanting more.

Our spirit is what makes us who we are and connects us to every other living creature in this world and the other side. Our spirit is the metaphysical body that allows us to be one with the universe and everything in it. And, our spirit allows us and even encourages us to tap in to and develop our psychic abilities.

Meditation

Just how stressed out are you? In a world where we want instant gratification, wouldn't you love an easy fix to alleviate some of that tension? Well, guess what? You can have it! Over the years, meditation has become seemingly more accessible to everyone. It used to feel like the only way meditation was available to the average layperson was to sign up with a personal guru or join some type of commune. But individual or group meditation can be done by all, anywhere. We are all able to reap the amazing benefits meditation offers. From a feeling of general relaxation to a deeper connection with the other side, meditation provides us with the basis to not only live a spiritual and mindful life but to be healthier and happier.

Meditating has many practical advantages. It can help balance your immune system, which will make you feel better. It can relax every aspect of your mind and body, which will contribute to an improved lifestyle. It can unite you with your spirit, which will allow you to access who you truly are. And it can help you connect to your intuition, which is crucial to leading a fuller, more perceptive life.

• EXERCISE 6 •
Meditate

Get comfortable. You are going to need at least ten minutes to do this meditation, so be sure you are somewhere you will not be disturbed.

Begin by breathing deeply a few times. Now open and close your eyes, and continue blinking until your eyes are ready to stay comfortably closed. Take another deep breath.

Feel the air around you lightening, allowing you to feel lighter. Feel a coolness as it slowly travels up your body, starting from the bottoms of your feet, moving through you and out of the top of your head. Feel that cool energy as it surrounds you like a bubble.

Imagine this bubble gently moving you toward a beautiful meadow. As you travel through the meadow, you can see flowers of every color: red, orange, yellow, green, blue, indigo, and violet. Now, the bubble gently rises up, bringing you into the white, fluffy clouds. You gradually float higher, above Earth's atmosphere, and into the universe, safely in the bubble. Look around and see the colors of the universe: blue, indigo, silver, white, and violet.

Breathe, taking in the variety of hues around you. Take another breath and inhale the vitality of the stars and the energy of the space between worlds. On the next breath out, reach toward the other side, the place where all is known and everything is love. As you inhale again, receive a never-ending bond that will always be with you, accessible whenever you need to connect to your intuition. Imagine you can see this connection like music notes on a staff as it flexes and grows, flowing calmly to you and through you.

Acknowledge the energy of the universe, now present within you, as you float freely and gradually back down through the clouds, safely coming back through the meadow and into your bubble where you sit or lay. As you breathe in and out, begin wiggling your fingers and toes. When you feel you are completely back in your body, you can open your eyes. As you do, acknowledge this new bond to the universe and your incredible intuition by giving thanks. Say aloud, "Thank you!"

Symbolic Messages

Symbolism is present throughout every area of our lives. Think about marketing and brand recognition. The golden arches are synonymous with McDonald's, and more broadly, fast food. FedEx is known as a nationwide delivery service and Google is recognized as a huge Internet search engine. We receive symbolic messages in much the same way to help us understand and identify what the communication means. For example, if we dream about a FedEx truck pulling into our driveway, chances are it suggests we are receiving something; whether it is a message or a package is yet to be determined.

I watched a short video where Deepak Chopra talked about the mind itself not playing much of a part with your intuition; there is too much thinking. Thinking involves analyzing, and thinking is not awareness. The perception of the thought voids the actual intuitive awareness. This essentially means that once you begin questioning your intuitive and psychic gifts, you will have a hard time believing in them. If you have to think about it too much, it can become difficult and you tend to get in your own way. But the mind does help interpret the messages you are receiving by deciphering what the information means or what the psychic chatter is, as with psychic symbolism. Your helpers will send messages that you will recognize, like the FedEx truck, to help you receive their communications in the easiest way possible.

There are some basic symbols taken from a kind of universal vault that are widely recognized. For example, seeing a stop sign in your mind's eye is pretty simple to interpret—it means to stop what you are doing or cease from moving forward. Or if you hear a telephone ringing, it's usually symbolic of someone trying to get in touch with you or even with the other side reaching out to you. Recognizing the common symbols as well as developing and identifying your own personal symbols allows you to tune in to your psychic abilities more easily than ever before.

• EXERCISE 7 •
Your Chest of Symbols

Take a moment to calm yourself; do "exercise 6" if necessary. When you are ready, close your eyes. Imagine a golden chest, opened, resting right above your head and floating, almost touching your hair, tickling your scalp. Envision this chest as a sieve funneling all of your psychic communications from the universe before they reach you. See the colors and the hinges and the clasp that is used to lock the chest shut.

Inside the chest are symbols sent from the universe to help you understand future messages. For each symbol you access, you can envision what it means to you. Using some basic symbols below, allow the image, thought, or feeling of the symbol to become personal and be meaningful to you as an individual. It is in this way that you will develop your own chest of interpretable messages,and you will remember what each one means if you receive them from the other side.

Take as much time as you need to fully recognize each object or emotion from the list below. Imagine it in full color, whatever it is. You may feel it, see it, smell it, or even hear what it's called in a certain way. Allow yourself to describe each object in full detail. As you watch in your mind's eye, the symbolic objects flow down into the chest after you've defined each one.

Symbolic Objects

ANGRY	FLOWERS	MUSIC	EMOTION
BIRTHDAY	FUTURE	OLD AGE	FATHER
BOOK	GUN	OUTDOORS	FEMALE
CANDLE	HAPPY	PICTURE	MALE
CAR	HOME	SAD	MARRIAGE
COMPUTER	INSIDE	SCHOOL	MOTHER
COUPLE	LETTER	SIBLING	SPOUSE
DIVORCE	LIGHT	SINGER	TELEVISION
DOG	LOVE	SPORTS	TREES

The chest is filling with symbolic information that you can use to interpret future symbolic messages. When you are all done, you may notice more items or feelings coming through. Take advantage of these, acknowledge them, and let them flow into your chest.

When you are all done, close the chest. When you need to interpret symbolic messages, you can open the chest at any time. If you are feeling stuck and having a hard time understanding what you are getting in the future, you have total access to your chest and can redo this exercise.

You can add to your psychic symbols chest at any time to develop vast and personal symbolic interpretations.

Chakras

Chakras are our spiritual charging points. They are the energy centers we have that regulate and help balance our spiritual bodies or our ethereal bodies. They also help control our physical and mental bodies as well. We have seven of these spiritual batteries, beginning at the base of our spine and running in a line to the top of our head. The word *chakra* comes from an ancient Indian language known as Sanskrit and translates roughly to "spinning wheels." These spinning wheels help us link to the universal energy that's all around us.

Each of the seven basic chakras has a purpose. Their jobs vary from chakra to chakra, as do their colors. Imagine them as rotating wheels or flowers that can be cleared of debris or negative energy. When they are spinning freely, they make us feel good. When they are clogged or unbalanced, it can cause discomfort in every possible way to our mind, body, or spirit. A basic summary of each is below, along with the possible outcomes of being balanced and unbalanced.

FIRST CHAKRA—ROOT

Location: base of spine

Color: red

Quality: responsible for our structure or foundation

When balanced: grounded and safe, contributes
to our financial security

When unbalanced: emotional or physical
insecurity can manifest financial insecurity
or instability, potential for unhealthy
relationship with food

SECOND CHAKRA—SACRAL

Location: a couple of inches below the belly
button or navel

Color: orange

Quality: responsible for our sensuality and
sexuality and our sense of connecting to
self and others

When balanced: creates a healthy feeling of
well-being, sense and sexuality, pleasure,
and creativity

When unbalanced: can cause sexual dysfunction or dissatisfaction, can create emotional imbalance, may create a lack of abundance, lack of creativity, may manifest in other sensory issues

THIRD CHAKRA——SOLAR PLEXUS

Location: solar plexus region, upper abdomen

Color: yellow

Quality: responsible for gut instinct, sense of power, strength, self-confidence, self-worth

When balanced: manifests in confident strength, helps intuition to flow, digestive system flows properly

When unbalanced: can cause a lack of self-esteem, digestive issues or discomfort, weight gain in belly area

FOURTH CHAKRA——HEART

Location: chest or heart area

Color: green

Quality: responsible for love, health, compassion, and healing

When balanced: manifests in love for oneself and the ability to love others, creates a peaceful, overall feeling of joy, creates healthy physical, spiritual and mental body

When unbalanced: can cause sadness, can manifest as illness in every aspect of your being, may create problems in or lack of relationships

FIFTH CHAKRA——THROAT

Location: neck and throat area

Color: blue

Quality: responsible for communication, clear hearing, or psychic hearing

When balanced: increase positive communications, conversations, and the ability to speak your truth and speak up for yourself, may help with clairaudient or psychic hearing abilities, can contribute to self-expression

When unbalanced: may manifest in thyroid problems, can cause an inability to speak your truth, may block psychic messages from being heard, may cause conformity over self-expression

SIXTH CHAKRA——THIRD EYE

Location: center of forehead

Color: indigo

Quality: responsible for clairvoyance, or clear psychic sight; seeing things clearly

When balanced: psychic vision may increase wisdom, can help with focus and the ability to see the big picture, can help with an active imagination

When unbalanced: may cut off psychic images from being recognized, can manifest in headaches or blurred vision, can cause scattered thoughts and ideas, may create an inability to make decisions

SEVENTH CHAKRA——CROWN

Location: top of head

Color: violet

Quality: responsible for connecting to the universe to receive messages, spiritual connections, psychic gifts

When balanced: can manifest in complete
joy and understanding, may increase the
messages from the other side, can provide
you with a feeling of elation, may add to
your feeling of clarity

When unbalanced: may throw off every other
chakra in the system, can block your
intuition, may create a sense of confusion

As with most everything in life, focusing on making something better can increase your happiness, and in this case, it can also improve your connection to the other side, thereby enhancing your psychic abilities. The first step to balancing your chakras, then, is focusing on each one to clear them and open them up. Luckily, you can do this with a simple meditation.

• EXERCISE 8 •
Clearing Your Chakras

Once again, take yourself to a tranquil location where you won't be disturbed. Get comfortable and unwind.

Begin by breathing deeply and closing your eyes. When you feel so incredibly relaxed, imagine yourself at the bottom of a path, a path that leads up toward the sky. There are seven natural platforms along the path.

When you are ready, take your first step onto the path. Feel your feet as they touch down on the earth. With each step now, feel your feet becoming more and more grounded as they connect with the dirt. Continue walking, gently stepping and feeling the bond of the center of the earth as its energy rises up to join to yours. As you continue to walk on the path, slowly up toward the first platform, allow your feet to stay grounded, attached to the earth by fluid roots that move with you.

You arrive at the first platform now, which is covered in beautiful red rose petals. Turn around slowly and notice how the red rose petals rise up and circulate around your body at the same level as the base of your spine. Enjoy the feeling of this beautiful red energy swirling around you, and even through you, balancing out your first chakra. When you are ready, continue up the path and make your way to the next platform, grounding yourself with each step you take.

Make your way to the center of the second platform, walking into orange daylily flowers. Move slowly in a circle as the lilies naturally surround your second chakra with their height at your navel. Feel the flowers balancing your sacral chakra as you move with them. When you feel comfortable, continue up to the next platform.

Once there, notice how extraordinary daffodils are flowing around your solar plexus area. Look down at your feet and see the yellow reaching up to your power center. Breathe into your abdomen as the flowers swirl around you and balance your third chakra. When you are ready, step off onto the path.

As you walk along, feel the earth's cleansing energy continuing to rise through the roots attached to your feet as it travels all the way up to your fourth chakra. Reaching your heart center, it joins with the platform of tall green grasses you've just entered. The grass waves around your chest area, balancing your heart chakra. Feel the healing green energy as it spins love and creates harmony. Continue on when you are ready.

Moving further up the path, continue grounding with the energy of the earth as you step onto the next platform, the blue platform. Breathe deeply as beautiful blue hydrangeas reach up and surround your fifth chakra. Your throat is tickled by the amazing blue flowers as they balance and clear any debris that is holding you back from speaking your truth or from hearing your messages. Continue to breathe in the blue until you feel comfortable moving forward.

Walking toward the next platform, you feel lighter and more in tune with your energy. Your third eye, or sixth chakra, is wide open now as a beautiful wild indigo plant blows around your forehead area. Feel this amazing indigo color as it blends and balances your psychic vision chakra. Imagine this area opening up as any negativity falls back down through the branches into the earth to be recycled into positive energy. When you feel your sight is cleared, it's time to continue on your way toward your last platform.

Stepping onto your final platform, you can feel soft violets floating down on the top of your head. Your crown chakra is filling up and swirling with the flowers as they balance and clear your seventh chakra. Feel a tingling sensation as your crown area is filling with positive energy and opening to the universe. You know now that you will receive messages with clarity.

Take another deep breath and once again feel the energy of the earth as it rises up, mixing with the newly balanced energy of your seven chakras. See the colors as the energy rises up through your red root chakra, orange sacral chakra, yellow solar plexus chakra, green heart chakra, blue throat chakra, indigo third eye chakra, and finally your violet crown chakra. Inhale deeply once more and open your eyes as you exhale, balanced and clear!

୭ଦ

Now that you're acquainted with your chakra system, you can expect to receive messages in new ways. Each chakra will play a part in interpreting your communications from the other side. You may feel an increase in your connection now, as your chakras are more balanced, which creates a better intuitive conveyance system. Be ready!

Auras

Don't rub your eyes … you may really be seeing auras. An aura is the manifestation of light and color that emanates from all living things. It is the energy that connects us throughout the universe. Auras are linked to our chakra system, the energy centers that are a huge rainbow part of our etheric bodies. Auras can tell us a lot about someone. We can sense weak spots in the aura, which can suggest physical or mental issues. Alternatively, we are able to identify points of power and strength by recognizing the brighter areas and the variety of colors present.

One of my friends has a really hard time physically, and she has for quite a while. Basic movements can cause her grief. She had surgery on her back many, many years ago to help with an issue, but the surgery just seemed to create a whole bunch of other problems. Knowing what I do, she asked me one day if I could figure out what was happening to cause her so much pain. I felt her aura. I tuned in and paid specific attention to where I felt any deficiencies. I psychically observed a void in her neck area and told her there was a lot of pain throughout her body that was actually stemming from her neck and that if they could relieve the pressure, it would help to alleviate her pain.

She went to the doctors soon after for an appointment she already had scheduled before I told her what I was getting from her energy. The doctor confirmed what I had read from her aura. Many of her problems were indeed coming from her neck. They would try to devise a plan to help her.

There are psychics who focus specifically on scanning the body. They are medical intuitives, and they read the energy of the aura and the chakras to discover what is missing or what could help their client. Psychically tuning in to someone's aura can allow a glimpse into the physical, mental, spiritual, and emotional energetic bodies for any inconsistencies and illnesses and other influences affecting their health and well-being. Auras are not static; they change constantly. Depending upon what we are doing or thinking, our aura continually ebbs and flows and the colors will morph into others. This is normal and to be expected. We can also push or pull our auras. When we experience extreme emotions, we have a tendency to push out our energy field. When we are happy, our auras tend to expand, almost reaching out to others. Alternatively, if we are sad or need some space, we retract our auras in toward our own bodies. And if we are afraid, we pull in to help protect ourselves. We can learn to work with auras by connecting to people's energy.

• EXERCISE 9 •
Working Your Aura

You can do this exercise with someone else or by yourself. Start by doing each step individually. You can be anywhere you'd like, but you will need to concentrate. Decide whether you'd like to stand up, sit, or lie down. Once you're done, take a few deep breaths and, if you're comfortable, close your eyes.

Now, focus on something that makes you feel really, really sad. It can be something personal or just something you've heard about. When you get absorbed by the emotion, notice how your body feels. Can you feel your aura retreating, pulling in? You may even feel kind of a heaviness surrounding you. When you are done, think of a blue sky until you feel neutral again.

Next, take it up a notch. Think of something that makes you extremely angry. Don't hurt yourself or anyone else, but focus on that feeling. Does it feel like you are pushing your energy out? It might even feel like you are directing or even shooting your aura toward someone or something that made you feel that way. Pay attention to how it feels to spread your energy out like this, then go back to neutral.

One more time, think of something that makes you over-the-top happy. It could be a relationship, a newborn baby, winning the lottery, or something personal that makes you ecstatic. Notice how it feels as your body changes direction and fills with joy. Do you feel yourself wanting to express that happiness? Does it feel like your energy expands around you? Once you've discovered how your aura reacts to feeling happy, go back to neutral by focusing on the image of a blue sky.

If you are doing this exercise with someone else, have them try to intuit which emotion you are experiencing by sensing your aura. Have your partner put their hands about an inch from you and work all the way around you and up and down, feeling your energy.

Then switch roles. How did each of you do? Did you know which emotion was affecting your auras? Was one better than the other? You can practice this any time you want in the future to get you back in touch with your aura!

As you can tell, auras can be easily manipulated. It is up to you to be able to identify what it feels like and to notice what it tells you. Auras also emanate in color, so you may notice you observe different colors around people, including yourself. Try to discern what colors you see and how they make you feel. By connecting the emotion and feeling of the aura with the color, you will be able to better translate what it means using your intuition.

Sparks

Sometimes I see sparks. Truly. These sparks appear to fly out of my client's heads as they get excited about something I've told them. They also soar out of their hearts when I connect them to their deceased loved ones. This is not because they are on fire. Rather, the sparks are the concentrated and enthusiastic bits of energy that build up when we are passionate about something. Very similar to static electricity, these pops of energy can feel like little electric shocks. You can think of them as little bursts of excited psychic flashes.

These bits of energy are not internal combustibles flying out of someone; they are energy that is manifesting. This energy carries information as well. When you are trying to tune in to your intuition to read someone else, these sparks are something you can virtually grab. They carry so much information because they are highly charged with emotion or passion. Like our auras, they project out. Unlike our auras, they are not always present, so if you're able to pick up on them, consider yourself extremely lucky!

By using your mind, body, and spirit connection, you've accessed your psychic gifts and connected to the universal energy. By tuning in to your etheric body (chakras and auras), you are able to expand your own personal energy to connect to others and perceive data psychically. You now have the knowledge to change your own energy by focusing and clearing your chakras when needed, even daily. This will inevitably assist you with developing your psychic abilities even further!

TIPS

- Slow your roll! Take just one minute to relax and meditate, and it will provide you with benefits for hours.

- Comprehending psychic messages becomes much easier when we recognize the symbolic information we are receiving.

- You can easily increase your happiness by balancing your chakra system.

- You can change how you feel by simply expanding your aura!

Chapter Three

UNDERSTANDING YOUR BASIC PSYCHIC GIFTS

Psychic gifts are plentiful. Not only is there an unlimited supply of psychic energy available for you to tap in to, there are multiple psychic abilities you can use to do it. Just like Shrek's onion comparison to the layers of ogres, psychic abilities can be layered up as well. I like to think of them like Napoleon pastries (cake-like pastry that is created by layering different custards, creams, and jams between pastry sheets). You can access your psychic gifts together without breaking them down by type just like you can take a bite of a Napoleon and the different ingredients join together to provide a harmonious taste. However, you can pull apart the layers of a Napoleon and each one gives you a delicious flavor, similar to breaking down each type of psychic ability, which can be combined but also successfully utilized individually by component.

Aren't They All the Same?

Psychic gifts are not all the same. There are many types of psychic abilities, but some tend to be more prevalent than others. There are four main psychic abilities; some you may be familiar with, and some you may relate to but don't know by name. Clairvoyance, clairaudience, clair-cognizance, and clairsentience are the most common. So, how do you know if you utilize these senses? Understanding what each one entails will help you determine whether you use it already or not.

Clairvoyance: Seeing Clearly

One of the most frequently misused terms when talking about psychic abilities is clairvoyance. Clairvoyance means clear seeing, from the Latin term *clair*, meaning "clear." This is one metaphysical gift. Many people use the word clairvoyant interchangeably with psychic, when in actuality it is merely one aspect of being psychic. In other words, being psychic does not necessarily mean you are clairvoyant, but being clairvoyant may indicate you have some psychic ability. Clairvoyance can be present in a couple of forms. The first and most common is to see in your mind's eye, or third eye, an image that is not physically there. The second form of psychic sight is to physically see outside of your mind, in the material world, someone or something that is not only visible to you psychically, but externally.

You may be predominately clairvoyant if:

- You see images in your mind.
- You have detailed dreams that you remember seeing.
- You see deceased loved ones.
- You see images when you are using your imagination.
- You see colors when tuning in.
- You say "I see you doing . . ." or "I see it being . . ." when answering questions.

Many people think clairvoyance means to see something the same way you would see the book in front of you or the furniture you are sitting on. But for the most part, it is about seeing in your mind's eye, or third eye, and only seeing bits and pieces. For example, you may see a school desk but not the entire school, or you may see the form of a woman but not the entire or even actual woman. Symbolically, you may see a cup of water to represent a pool or an image of just water to represent an ocean (see chapter 2: Energy, Meditation, and Symbols). By asking for clarity with the vision, you may receive more, but often you will have to decipher what it means for you.

I was driving to Washington, D.C., recently with a new friend, Nicole. We were discussing what I do. She was very interested and curious about my process, and I could tell she wanted to know if I was picking up on anything for her.

"So, when you do readings, how does it work?"

This is probably one of the questions I hear most—well, that and "Are you reading my mind right now?" to which I jokingly answer, "Why, YES! Of course!" Even though I'm not.

"It depends on the reading and the client," I answered truthfully.

"Well, I mean, how do you know if you are connecting with someone or if someone is trying to tell you something?"

"If I'm doing an actual reading, I have to trust that pretty much everything I'm getting is from someone who is psychically trying to tell me something about the client. If I'm not doing a reading, I usually just shut that part down so I can be present," I replied, knowing of course she was trying to be good and not pester me.

I don't usually just offer up information, but I could tell she was really interested and hoping to receive some type of message, so I did a quick tune in as she was driving us on the Beltway.

"Is there an 'M' name for you? Someone you were very close to?"

"I don't think so," she answered, both excited and disappointed at the same time.

"I'm getting an 'M.' I am also getting something about water?"

"Nope. Not sure what any of that means," she responded thoughtfully. She seemed a little bummed that I was not connecting to anyone she could recognize.

"I am hearing something about swimming or a pool? Or someone who did water aerobics or exercise?" I continued, knowing I was on to something because I couldn't shake the image of water and I kept feeling like it was exercise.

"No, still nothing. Ah, well, that's okay. Thanks for trying!" she said, definitely a bit deflated but still a touch hopeful.

"Hmmm. Did you have a little dog? A dog named Max that used to swim or exercise in the water because he was sick?"

"OH MY GOODNESS! Yes! I absolutely did! I loved Max so much! He got me through a lot of tough times!"

"Great! So why am I seeing the water aerobics? And did he have something wrong, like Lyme or some other debilitating disease?" I continued.

"Yes! He did aqua therapy due to degeneration from Lyme disease. He used to run on a treadmill under water! He absolutely loved it!" she replied, with unexpected tears coming down her face.

"Wow! But that's not what killed him, though it's connected to that, right?"

"Right! We were getting out of the car for therapy and he was so excited he jumped out of my minivan and broke his back! It was devastating. But I loved that little dog. He was so incredibly special and important to me! Thank you so much!"

"Just know his energy is always with you, and he laughs about the cat," I told her.

"HA! We do have a cat now! And, yes, I believe Max would be cracking up about that!" she answered, her curiosity and desire totally satiated because her best furry friend had come through for her.

You will rarely receive the images playing out like a movie on a screen. More often than not it will be more like snapshots, usually kind of blurry. Or even, taking it further, ripped and blurry snapshots because you won't have the full picture. What I saw for Nicole was not exactly what happened or who her actual connection was. I received pieces of it and was able to put it together using these clues. At first I wasn't even aware it was a dog. Although this did come through eventually, in the beginning it was just an energy that she could connect to which I knew shared a mutual love. After we discovered who it was, she told me about just how close she was with Max and it made the whole experience I was having fit. Don't ever discount the information you are being shown, just try to figure out where it may belong by assembling the different parts.

• EXERCISE 10 •
Seeing Clearly

Training yourself to see in your mind's eye is one way to help your clairvoyant abilities expand. A simple way to do that is to use your imagination. Close your eyes and take a deep breath. You may have to breathe a couple of times to slow yourself down. You want to relax your body, mind, and spirit. Once you've relaxed, you are ready to begin. Take your time, and remember there is no right or wrong answer.

Now, in your mind's eye—that place inside your head where you will see things using your clairvoyance— imagine a dog. Notice first what color the dog is. Next, pay attention to whether you see the whole dog or just a part of the dog. Expand your vision to see the whole dog if you didn't already. Notice if there are any unusual markings on the dog. Does it have fur? If so, is it fluffy or short or in-between? Is it wearing a collar or even a dog-gie sweater? Can you tell if it is a male or female? Is the dog sitting, standing, or lying down? Can you tell if the dog is friendly or not? Though the main reason for this exercise is to utilize your clairvoyance, you may also pick up on any feelings you get around the dog. For example, are you drawn to the dog or are you afraid of the dog or neutral? Finally, can you tell what kind of dog breed it is?

When you have seen everything you can imagine, open your eyes. Think about how clearly you were able to see the dog in your mind's eye. Did it feel natural? Was it difficult? The place in your mind where you are able to envision the dog is the same place you will receive clairvoyant messages.

Let's take it one step further. Close your eyes again and focus on that empty space in your imagination and let it fill now with the image of the next dog you will see with your physical eyes. (If you have a dog, don't let that be the one we are talking about—that would be too easy!) Intuit in your mind's eye the next dog you will see. It may be on the television or the computer or even outside. Just try to envision what the dog will look like. Make note of any details, as you did above. When you are done, open your eyes.

Check in with yourself after you actually physically see a dog. Were you on point? Did you physically see the dog you saw in your mind's eye? Were there similarities in size or shape or color? Do you feel you matched the image in your mind's eye to the physical dog well, or were you totally off?

Use this exercise any time you want to expand your clairvoyant abilities. You can try it with cats or cars or houses or even people. The important thing is to recognize where your clairvoyant space is in your mind's eye and how to train your imagination or your psychic vision to see with more detail. The more you can imagine, the better your clairvoyance will be!

ᕙᕗ

Psychic vision will not always present you with a clear or a full picture. More often than not you will only see small bits of whatever it is you are tuning in to. Using your thoughts, as well as your imagination, you can piece together whatever the message or the imagery is. Allow your imagination to play an active role in your clairvoyant experience. At times it will be difficult to separate the two, but with practice you will be able to understand the difference.

Claircognizance: What Do You Know?

Claircognizance is clear knowing. It's when you know something that you have no reason to know and no physical evidence to prove it, but you still just know it. It is a definitive answer in your mind—being aware of something with absolute certainty, without a logical explanation as to why.

You might be predominately claircognizant if:

- You know things, but you don't know why you know them.
- You know something is off, for no apparent reason, without evidence.
- You just know whether someone is moving in the right direction.
- You know if someone is being honest or lying without evidence.
- You know someone is doing the right or wrong thing.
- You know who is calling before you see caller ID or answer the phone.
- When talking with someone, you tend to say, "I know what you mean."

Often people will ask me questions that require yes or no answers. If it's something that I can give rapid-fire answers to, then I will use my claircognizance. I don't process the question, I just say what comes psychically and instantly. I just *know* the answer. When you analyze the question or try to navigate through the answer, it is no longer claircognizance. It may be psychic, as you might be using other intuitive abilities, but thinking about it to try to figure it out in some way negates the knowing.

Before my mom died, we wanted to move her either into our house or some type of assisted living facility. The problem with this was she did not want to move. Though she was disabled, she retained all of her mental faculties. She was also a retired critical care head nurse so she was somewhat capable of taking care of her own bed ridden self and knew she didn't want to give up control to anyone. So, when I did a reading for her and tried to see where she would move, all I knew claircognizantly was there would be a big pine tree overlooking wherever she was. I just knew, not seeing anything or hearing anything, but knowing that old pine tree would be there.

A couple years later my mom passed. We had her funeral and then drove in procession to the cemetery. When we arrived, we discovered the cemetery employees had mistakenly dug up my in-law's burial site. They thought that we didn't just want a plot in the vicinity of where my husband's parents were, but instead, for some crazy reason, they thought we wanted my mom buried in the same actual grave. I can tell you this did not go over too well; the wound of my wonderful mother- and father-in-law's passing was still fresh. After hours of communicating with many different employees, they finally realized their mistake and also admitted they had no plots left. Great. This was already difficult enough.

When my mother died, I originally wanted her buried in another part of the cemetery, where my great-grandparents and grandparents had a plot. But for some reason my family had felt it wasn't a good idea to ask my grandparents. Now there was no choice. They called them, as they themselves had been unable to travel the four hours to get home due to illness, and they affirmed what I originally thought—my mom should absolutely be buried in the family plot.

After many hours and many tears, my mom was finally laid to rest in the middle of a beautiful, large, parklike cemetery. As we were getting ready to leave, I knelt down to touch the ground to say goodbye. I looked up and saw, for the first time, a huge pine tree immediately looking over her gravesite. I glanced around the rest of the cemetery and saw the rest of the trees were oaks or maples. No huge pines stood out—except for the one I had known she would be looked over by when we finally moved her to a new location.

Even though I knew claircognizantly that she would move somewhere, that there would be a huge pine tree, I had no idea what else it meant. I assumed at the time that we would be able to convince her to move somewhere more amenable to her needs, but I was wrong. She did move, but it was her last one in this lifetime. And it turned out to be in a beautiful spot surrounded by family and protected by an incredibly amazing pine tree.

Just knowing something doesn't mean you will always receive conformation regarding objects or even people. It may not explain in depth what your claircognizance is telling you. But, as I wrote earlier, claircognizance is a great way to answer basic yes and no questions.

• EXERCISE 11 •
Just Know

Grab your pen and journal. It's time to answer some questions! For this exercise I want you to trust in your claircognizant sense and simply write down yes or no or basic one-word answers to the questions that follow. Do this without thinking about them at all or actually processing the words.

- Will you be married happily ever after?
- Will you travel soon?

- Are you content?
- Are you in the right job?
- Should you change careers?
- Are you in a positive relationship?
- Is there life after death?
- Have you lived before?
- What was your name?
- Name one person who will be influential in your life over the next year.
- Have you ever had a psychic flash?
- Are you intuitive?
- Will your financial structure be good over the next year?
- Is this the best book for you right now?
- Are your deceased loved ones around you?
- Do you have spirit guides?
- Who helps you from the other side?
- Is there a reason you are here?
- Should you develop your psychic abilities further?
- Are you destined for greatness?

How'd it go? Did you feel your claircognizance kick in? It's possible you over thought the answers. Don't be too hard on yourself. You can practice this on your own by asking more random questions that are immediately verifiable, like what will be on the television when you turn it on? Who is the first person you'll see when you walk into school or work or the store?

Obviously these are just a sampling of questions, so you can add more. You can also practice with a friend by having them ask you rapid-fire questions. Turn it into a game and make it fun. Using your intuition should never feel like a task; it should always be enjoyable. It may be difficult at times, but if you get too stressed it will work against you. It will actually become counterintuitive!

Clairsentience: Can You Feel It?

Similar to claircognizance and often going hand in hand is clairsentience, or clear feeling. This is the gut instinct you have or the gentle nudging telling you to go in a specific direction or even stopping you from doing something. Perhaps the prodding that's keeping you moving though everyone is telling you it is not the right way for you. It's the feeling you get when someone is just not right or a situation seems off. You can experience a sensation of being physically sickened by this clairsentient feeling. Some people may even become nauseated when presented with what they intuitively sense as negative or feel elated if they interpret it as a positive vibe.

You may also become more aware of this sense during mediumship (or talking with people that have passed). When deceased people show up, they will often make you feel as though you are walking through spider webs.

This psychic phenomenon can occur for more than one person in tandem as well. My husband and I regularly experience it together when we are discussing our parents who have passed. We can be walking in a grocery store and all of a sudden we will both look at each other and rub our faces and arms and ask each other at the same time, "Did you just walk through a web?" We then become aware that not only are our relatives visiting, but they are letting us know they appreciate us.

Body awareness, or a heightened awareness of your body, plays a big role in interpreting clairsentient messages. Keeping your body healthy, getting enough sleep, eating properly, and exercising on a regular basis will help you in every aspect of developing your psychic abilities, but it is especially crucial when needing your body to feel your intuition.

Clairsentience is very similar to claircognizance. Some of the markers are very similar. You might find you excel at clairsentience if:

- You can feel when things are off.
- You feel when someone is lying to you.
- You can tell when a situation feels right or wrong.
- You feel someone else's energy and can tell if they are a good person or not.
- When expressing yourself, you tell people, "I feel ... "
- You tend to follow your gut instincts.

I was doing a reading for Cheryl recently. I was tuning in and giving her all of the information I was getting as it came in. During the reading, however, I kept experiencing pains in my ovaries. It felt like sharp, stabbing pains, and at first I didn't acknowledge them out loud because I thought it was just my own body acting out. As the session continued, I realized I had to ask Cheryl if she had any issues with her own reproductive area.

"Nope. Nothing," she answered.

"Okay. I'm feeling really strong pains. I don't think it's that time of the month for me ... " I let it trail off as I contemplated the pain some more.

I kept going through the reading. Other topics were being discussed, all the while I had this unrelenting pain that I could feel in my ovarian area.

"Do you know someone who passed of ovarian or uterine cancer? Or someone with a 'D' name?" I asked her. I knew there was something strange going on.

"No, no idea. Sorry!" Cheryl answered.

"Okay." I laughed and began wrapping up the reading.

"Wait," I continued as she was getting ready to leave.

As she turned and looked I asked her if there was someone she knew who was "quirky" or was known for being quirky or something. I got a huge stabbing pain that made me bend over.

"Wow. I think I get it! I will have to confirm, but my friend's last name is Quirk. Her friend Deb just passed two weeks ago from what I believe was ovarian cancer," she answered, excited to have figured out who was coming through but saddened she had passed.

"Just know that Deb is trying to let her friend know she is good on the other side," I told her, and the pain I had been experiencing immediately subsided.

I received a text almost immediately after our session letting me know that her friend, whose last name was Quirk, did indeed lose her friend Deb to ovarian cancer. Deb was using any way she possibly could to get through to her friend who was grieving here. She used my body and allowed me to feel her cause of death by using my clairsentient sense. If I hadn't mentioned it to Cheryl, we wouldn't have been able to pass along her message of love.

That said, you want to be able to control how you receive information. Learning to use the energy of other people without letting it take over your energy is a significant part of tuning in with your clairsentient gifts. Otherwise you won't ever be able to determine whether it is a message or intuitive hit you are picking up or if it's just something you are personally experiencing. Recognizing what energy feels like will help to key you in.

• EXERCISE 12 •
Feel the Energy

It's time to identify your energy. Place your hands in front of you, palms facing each other. Focus your attention on the space between your palms. Gently bounce your hands back and forth toward each other and away from each other, feeling the energy in between. In the beginning, you may notice you begin to feel something when you reach the space the size of a golf ball. Pulse your hands in and out until you can clearly feel the energy.

When you are aware of it, try to expand the energy out to the size of a grapefruit. Continue outward, going as large as you can until you no longer feel it, then move your hands back in again until you do.

Try this with a friend! Place your palms directly out in front of you, facing your partner's. Practice feeling each other's energy by pulsing your hands together and apart. Then, take turns closing your eyes, having the other person move just one of their hands. Open your eyes and tell your partner which hand you believe was moving based on how the energy felt to you.

Were you able to determine the correct hand? Did you feel the energy? Was your partner able to feel your energy? How did it feel for you to do this with a partner versus by yourself? Was it stronger or less identifiable? Which did you prefer? You can also try it with a couple of friends. Take turns closing your eyes and having one friend step up. Try to determine whose energy you are dealing with before you open your eyes. Were you able to? Were your friends? How did it feel? Could you feel the difference?

Clairaudience: Listen Up!

More often than not, that voice in your head is there to help you, not because you are experiencing a psychotic break (though if you need help, seek out a medical professional). What you may be experiencing is clairaudience. Clairaudience, or clear hearing, often seems like something you're making up. You may hear sounds inside your mind, which can be confusing at first. It is normal to question whether you are hearing with your psychic ears or if you are just imagining it. These internal sounds may be voices that are clearly sending you words you can recognize or they may be fuzzy. You may also hear sounds or music. For example, if you are trying to decide whether to take a car, a boat, a plane, or a train to go on vacation, and you hear a train whistle, you can be assured you've just received your answer.

How do you know if you might be clairaudient?

- You learn by saying things out loud or listening to others.

- Music tends to speak to you—you love to sing, play instruments, and turn to music for comfort.

- Ideas are born or sorted out from what seems like voices in your head.

- You find yourself hypersensitive to noise—always trying to work out exactly what you are hearing.

- You receive answers to your questions vocally; you hear them.

- You express yourself by saying, "I hear you . . ."

"Discus of the Gods" is what I heard during a session with Tina.

Having said that, I have to explain I was talking to my client Tina about her kids. I saw everything was going well, and they were doing well in school. Then I asked my guides if there was anything specific they were doing and I heard "Discus of the Gods," so I told Tina, laughing. I had absolutely no idea why I was hearing this until Tina cleared it up for me.

"That is so funny! My son just created an ultimate fris-bee league at his school. He has his first game next week!" she replied.

Now I understood. So I continued my reading with her. It wasn't until weeks later when I received a message from her that she was able to validate a few other things that I had apparently told her during her reading. She reminded me of how it went.

I had told her, "I see something or someone connected to you that has to do with California."

"I don't think so. I can't think of any California connections," Tina had answered.

Tina has had readings with me before. She knows that the information I give her usually has meaning at some point, so she was willing to hold on to the California thing for future reference. I knew I would forget soon after, as I always do—I never remember information from readings.

"Alright. I'm also getting something about Georgia. I think it has to do with your work. Are you getting a job there? I am hearing 'commuting to Georgia from Connecticut,' which doesn't make any sense, but I have to give it to you as I get it!" I told her.

"That works! I am interviewing for a job in Atlanta," she responded.

"Oh darn. Not sure what the Georgia reference is, then," I said, a bit perplexed because I was sure I had heard Georgia for her.

"What do you mean? You're pulling my leg, right?" Tina laughed.

"Umm, no? I did—I heard Georgia. Not Atlanta," I admitted.

"You do realize where Atlanta is, right?" she asked, confused but still laughing.

"Oh, wow! Oops! I was so focused on Georgia I wasn't thinking. Of course I know Atlanta is in Georgia. Well, you are going to have to let me know if you get the job," I told her, feeling silly.

Tina messaged me a couple weeks later.

"I figured out the California connection you mentioned in my reading, and you're good!" she wrote.

I messaged back, "Woohoo! Thanks. What was it?"

"My replacement is coming from California," she shared.

"Oh, well that makes sense then. But wait, your replacement?" I responded, a bit nervous for her. I hoped she hadn't gotten fired or something.

"Yes! It's a good thing. I got the job in Atlanta. Remember, Georgia?"

I could practically hear the laughter as I read her message. I was happy for her. It reminded me that although I received the communication clairaudiently, and I'd only received a few words to go by, it wasn't crucial for me to understand it completely. It was all right that I just gave her what I received instead of trying to figure out what I was receiving. Time was her friend and everything unfolded the way it was supposed to.

• EXERCISE 13 •
Can You Hear It?

You may or may not be predominately clairaudient, but remember, either way is fine! One way to develop this ability is to listen to songs. Turn on the radio and try to decipher the words to the next five songs you hear. You may find that it is very easy or it may be more difficult. Training your physical ears to listen helps you to hear with greater clarity when you use your clairaudience.

Next, share your clairaudient abilities with a friend. Get together with someone who listens to or likes the same type of music. Take turns singing the songs in your mind. Using your clairaudience, try to hear what song the other is singing.

If you found this exercise to be difficult, that's okay. You can keep practicing. If it was easy, great! You may have a strong sense of clairaudience.

As with any psychic message, always trust in what you are receiving. That is the only way you will begin to really understand that you are getting intuitive information. If you don't acknowledge the sounds or the words you are hearing, you can never validate them.

TIPS

ᦕ

- There are enough psychic abilities to go around. Peel back each psychic layer to discover yours.

- Trust in what you see! Even if it feels like your imagination, it may really be a clairvoyant hit.

- Go with what you know.

- Listen up! Quiet yourself long enough to allow messages to come through.

- Those goose bumps you get may very well be a psychic nudge for you to pay attention to what you're feeling.

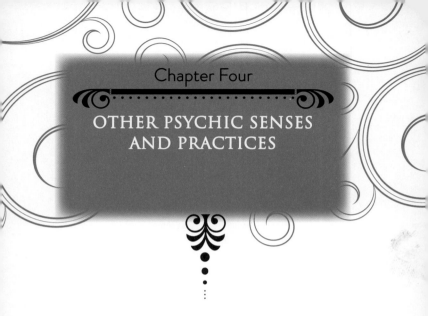

Chapter Four

OTHER PSYCHIC SENSES
AND PRACTICES

So far you've discovered the most widely recognized psychic senses. These are the senses most people will start their psychic journey with. These abilities are the prevalent ones, the gifts many naturally have to begin with. But, not to be overlooked are a few others. Sometimes known as helper clairs, clairempathy, clairgustance, clairolfaction (also known as clairalience or clairescence), and clairtangency all play their own roles when tuning into your psychic awareness. Telepathy, mediumship, and remote viewing are common ways of employing all of your psychic gifts in practical applications.

The Other Clairs

Clairempathy is similar to clairsentience in that it has to do with feeling, but clairempathy is more about feeling other's emotions. Becoming emotional in some way, even if it doesn't feel like your own emotions, may happen because you are taking on the feelings of someone else. You may experience what they are feeling, good or bad, without consciously recognizing that you are doing it. Regardless of whether it's feeling emotions or feeling something with your body, psychic feeling is a pretty common ability.

You may be an empath if:

- You feel the emotions other people are feeling.

- You get grumpy because someone you're nearby is, even though you were perfectly happy before they came in.

- You instantly develop the same or similar aches and pains as someone else around you or close to you.

- You often say, "I feel you ... "

• EXERCISE 14 •
Do You Feel It?

With this exercise you need a partner or, even better, a loved one. Sit on the floor (or in two separate chairs if the floor proves too difficult) with your backs to each other. Take a few deep breaths together, and when you are both relaxed, go ahead and close your eyes.

Have your partner think of an event or a person that causes them to experience a strong emotion. Allow that emotion to build for a moment. Have them really feel the emotion. Then, using your clairempathic gifts, try and intuit the emotion your partner is feeling. Allow the feeling to overcome your own emotions by focusing on their energy. Tell them what you think they are experiencing and be specific. Don't just say happy if you feel gleeful or mad if you are feeling rage. Don't beat yourself up if you don't hit it immediately. Many emotions overlap, depending upon the situation they are thinking about. Have them explain to you what they were feeling. You may find what you were feeling makes more sense to you by understanding their circumstance.

Try it again a few more times and then switch. Let your partner intuit what you are feeling. Mix it up by using different emotions. Are they able to pick up on what you're feeling? Who tuned in better? Did you notice you were able to feel one emotion stronger than another? For example, anger versus happiness? Whether you did well this time or not, keep practicing with other people and discover who it works best with. Usually people that we're close with will have a greater impact on us and will therefore help our clairempathy work at its full potential.

Clairgustance means clear tasting, and if you've ever tasted pickles you know exactly how that can work; I bet your mouth just watered. This means you taste things you're not actually eating. Usually these things are symbolic of someone who passed or something you used to do. For instance, if your great-grandmother was known for her key lime pie, and you all of a sudden taste it in your mouth, it may be a sign she's around you.

You may be proficient with your clairgustant sense if:

- The thought of a specific food transports you to a different time or place.

- You associate certain foods or tastes with specific people when they are brought up.

- Specific people make you taste a certain flavor in your mouth.
- You tend to associate food flavors with geographical locations.
- You get a nasty taste in your mouth when thinking of a bad situation or a specific person.
- You tend to say, "That gives me a bad taste," when asked about something.

• EXERCISE 15 •
Taste It

The first step to understanding your clairgustance is to determine what you are tasting. So, to help you do this, you need to use your imagination to allow you to psychically connect to the various flavors listed. Be sure to let yourself experience each one, even if it's something you don't care for. One at a time, take a moment to conjure up the flavor until you feel as though you are physically tasting it.

Flavors

| APPLES | WINE | PICKLES | LEMONS | OLIVES |
| COFFEE | CAKE | MEATBALLS | SHRIMP | TEQUILA |

When you are done, continue by thinking about other flavors. Remember, these flavors are your passport to clairgustance, so allow them to fill your entire mouth!

ༀ

Clairolfaction is clear smelling and is the sense you are utilizing when you smell the perfume of your deceased friend or the cigar of your late grandfather. Many people speak of the smell of flowers or even cookies baking when their grandmother comes through or fresh-cut grass when their dad shows up. You can also experience aromas to indicate someone who passed from disease or if someone is sick.

Haley came into my office a couple of years ago for a psychic reading. She wanted to know about her current relationship. She told me they were talking about getting married and wanted to know what I got from it. The problem was I was getting even more than that.

"I'm excited! I can see myself walking down the aisle! But ... " she said, letting the last bit trail off.

"I can feel his energy. Your fiancé seems like a great guy!" I responded, wondering what else was going on.

"I know! He really is," she answered. "I just have a strange feeling that I can't put my finger on."

"Hmmm. Let me tune in," I told her. "I like his energy. He seems like an honestly nice guy," I continued.

"Okay, I just don't know. There is something going on," Haley said.

I tuned in and tried to pick up on what she was saying. Everything felt good. I wasn't picking up any type of abuse or suspicious behavior. But then I began smelling something. To me, it smelled like my old cat, Matilda, who had passed away many years ago. I started to put it together.

"Has he been feeling well? Is he sick in some way?" I asked her.

"He has been having bad headaches. That's about it," she replied.

"I think he needs to go to the doctor for the headaches. I think there may be reason for your weariness," I shared. "Come back after he goes for an appointment."

A couple of weeks later she returned to my office to share what was happening.

"So, we took your advice and booked him an appointment with his doctor. They did some tests and realized there was a tumor. They didn't think it was cancerous, but they needed to remove it because it was causing pressure on his brain, which was causing the headaches. They even said if the tumor was allowed to continue growing, it could have killed him."

"I am so glad you took him for the tests! I knew something was wrong when I started smelling my cat, who was sick before she died. I was psychically smelling this scent when I tuned in to your fiancé. I am sending you both positive energy and congratulations on your upcoming wedding!"

I had used my clairolfaction, luckily, to tune in. Initially I was only using my other psychic senses. I did not intentionally use my clear-smelling sense but was grateful that my guides knew which senses to tickle in order to help Haley's fiancé.

You may connect to your clairolfactory senses predominately if:

- You sense loved ones around you through smell.

- You smell illness or disease on someone.

- You smell foods or vitamins that someone is lacking.

- You smell a foul odor to represent something that is not good for you or others.

• EXERCISE 16 •
Smell It

Similar to clairgustance, you need to practice discerning different scents to help you connect to your clairolfactory sense. Smell the following items in your mind:

Smells

CIGARS	CIGARETTES	ROSES	SWEAT	COOKING
GREASE	NATURE	DOG	POPCORN	MUSTY

Notice which scents are stronger for you. Are there some that make you think of a particular person—maybe someone who has passed or even someone who is still present? Pay attention to the different scents that stand out to you for a variety of people. These will be the scents you'll experience from now on when you think of them.

෨෨

Clairtangency is a little less employed and means clear touch. Clairtangency is when you touch an item and information is relayed that is associated with the item, like psychometry (see chapter 6: Other Ways to Connect). Various objects hold energy that can be transmitted and deciphered through a simple touch. Touching a person's hand or face can also stimulate your clairtangent gifts.

A variety of information can be gained through human touch, which is why you may notice many psychics ask to hold hands with the person they are reading for. Clairtangency helps to collect personal data from the one you are sitting with, such as what's happening with the person's career, health, and even who their family members are or what they are up to.

Being drawn to antiques may indicate something more than just an appreciation of all things old. It might be that you are drawn to the energy attached to the items. Most old objects have a history, and by touching the object you may be able to intuit a wealth of information about the former owners, or people who may have used the antique or even parties or events that took place where the object formerly was.

You might realize you are clairtangent if:

- You find yourself touching others often to feel closer to them (in a healthy way).

- You touch objects and feel their history.

- You are a hugger.

• EXERCISE 17 •

EXERCISE 17 •
Touch It

Work on this psychic sense by taking advantage of your friends. One by one touch their hand or their hair. Tell them what you feel. Do you get something about their life, or possibly what they did recently? Maybe a name or an initial of someone that is close to them, or even of someone who has passed? The sky is the limit. Tell them everything you get, psychically, without censoring it. Remember, what may mean nothing at all to you can mean everything to them!

Telepathy

Generally, the answer to the question "Are you reading my mind right now?" is no, but on occasion it just may be yes! Telepathy is the ability to know what someone else is thinking about. It's an interesting concept because unlike other psychic gifts, it can be a stand-alone ability for someone and can be easily proven. Telepathy is what you are using when you are able to intuit the number between 1 and 100 that someone else may be thinking. It's also there when out of the blue you and a friend say the exact same thing at the same time.

Telepathy can be like psychic spying. Can you imagine how you would feel if someone heard your thoughts? Interesting, right? This happens more often than we realize. Mental communication can become a somewhat regular thing among spouses or siblings. It also occurs with best friends. Twins tend to frequently send each other telepathic messages, too. My husband and I do it all the time, and we have yet to figure out who thought of whatever we are thinking of first.

A while back I was having a session with one of my regular clients, Sophie. She had come in for an appointment but we hadn't talked about what she wanted to do during the session. Being a regular, she took advantage of all I had to offer, including psychic readings, hypnosis, reflexology, Reiki, and even coaching. So, when we hadn't specified what she wanted to do for the upcoming hour, I decided to tune in to her thoughts. I knew from previous history that she thought about her needs and wants while driving to her session with me.

When Sophie came in it was with a rush of wind, as she was late. She had been daydreaming, she said, thinking about her appointment.

"So, I know we hadn't talked about what we were going to focus on this time, but I had an idea," she told me.

"Okay, what are you thinking?" I asked with a grin. I already knew what she was going to say.

"I would love for you to do a—" she began.

"Reading," I interrupted her.

"How did you know? I just thought about it on the drive over!" Sophie said incredulously.

I pulled out the paper I had done for her. Normally, before every reading, I tune in and write down whatever information comes to me, which is usually the basis for the entire reading. It opens us up to everything the universe has to share with my clients.

"I tuned in and read your mind! I used telepathy because I needed to know which direction we were going today," I told Sophie, confident that telepathy had indeed guided me to begin the reading before she had even walked through my office door.

You may have telepathic gifts if:

- You finish other people's sentences.

- You say the same thing someone else was about to say or at the same time.

- You call a friend or loved one while they are dialing your number.

- You hear in your mind what someone else is thinking.

- You have a thought out of the blue of what someone else is thinking

• EXERCISE 18 •
Do You Know What They Are Thinking?

For this exercise, you will again need the help of a friend. Have your partner think of a color. Have them repeat the color continuously in their mind while you relax and try and connect to their thoughts. Focus in and try to read their mind. Can you intuit the color they are thinking by using your telepathic gifts? You might notice a variety of psychic senses come in to help you out. That's totally fine. Telepathy can employ all of your gifts.

When you've done a bunch of different colors, try it with numbers, species of animals, or names. Pay attention to how well you do with each different category. Feel free to switch positions with each grouping. Does one of you work better as the sender or the giver? Take it to the next level and have a bunch of people think of the same thing while you try and read their minds. Who knows, it may turn into a telepathic party! Enjoy it.

Remote Viewing

Remote viewing is the ability to pick up information distant in both time and space. It is the gift of knowing about a person, place, or thing without being anywhere near them. It is very helpful when looking for a lost object and even with psychic detective work. Think about how great it would be if you were able to find a stolen car or even give law enforcement the location of a missing person. This can be done through remote viewing.

Remote viewing, as designed by the government in conjunction with scientists from the Stanford Research Institute, follows a very specific protocol. It was created without a typical psychic in mind, but rather a layperson who can imagine the possibilities. For all intents and purposes it was made to be accessible first by a secret department of the military and later by anyone who followed the exact directions. In my book *Psychic Vision: Developing Your Clairvoyant and Remote Viewing Skills,* I outline and describe each of the formal steps.

Remote viewing, without following all of the strict procedures, essentially is about using all of your gifts to tune in to something, distant in time and space, and gather information and bring it back to be assimilated. By using all of your intuitive gifts at once, you can get a better picture of what you are tuning in to. Remote viewing is especially good when you need to locate something.

Utilizing the basic design of remote viewing, the key is to tap into each of your psychic senses one at a time to locate a target. For example, let's say you are trying to find your lost bracelet. First use your clairvoyance. Ask the universe to *show* you where the bracelet is. You may see images of a blanket or even a bed. They may be symbolic images or you might actually see with your third eye the blankets or bed in your room. Then, *listen* to where it is using your clairaudience. If you're like me and have a fan going every night, maybe you hear a whirring, blowing sound in the background. Next, go ahead and *feel* where your bracelet is using your clairsentience. Because it's a bedroom you may feel sleepy or you may even feel sexy. If you continue tapping in to your different senses, one at a time, you will continue to gather all of the evidence needed to intuit where your bracelet is.

By now you would at least have an idea of what you've intuited so far. Often you may find that not all of your senses help you. But the benefit of using all of your gifts is that it works even if some don't provide you with the information you need. The whole point to remote viewing is to gather all of the data together so every piece of evidence can add to the entire target. Obviously, using this example, the target was the bracelet and by utilizing your different psychic abilities you were able to locate it as being somewhere in your bedroom. You can pinpoint it even further by collecting even more details using your intuitive senses.

Remote viewing does not limit you. In fact, it encourages you to expand your gifts as far as you can to assemble all of the pertinent information. Like baking a chocolate cake, there are many ingredients that are crucial to the final product. And, like baking, there are many different recipes. It is the combination and how they work together that produces the result.

• EXERCISE 19 •
Where Is It?

Practicing remote viewing is simple. Find something by intuiting where it is. You need only to decide what you want as your target. For me, it's my wedding ring. It may be a favorite tool or a pair of shoes—anything you've lost. I would hold off on trying to locate a missing person or a long-lost parent until you practice a bit on inanimate objects. So, once you've chosen what you are going to tune in to, take your journal to a quiet, comfortable space.

Close your eyes and take a deep breath. Imagine a silver waterfall of energy flowing over you from above, surrounding you and protecting you and opening you up to receive messages from the universe. Sit with this energy until you feel totally calm and relaxed.

Now, think about what you currently believe to be your dominant psychic ability. It may be clairvoyance, clairaudience, claircognizance, etc. Once you've determined which gift it is, decide on which is your next strongest. Go through all of the gifts you've read about so far in this book and write them down in order of strength. Don't get too crazy over it; the idea is just to begin with your most comfortable psychic abilities.

When you've written them down, you can begin. Flip to a fresh sheet of paper and write down the object you are trying to locate. Then, put your pen down and close your eyes and focus on the first gift you've listed. If it's clairvoyance, tune in using your psychic sight. What images come to mind? What pictures do you see? Remember, just write down what you see. Don't try to figure out exactly what it is you are looking at.

Continue with each psychic ability, recording the information you perceive as you go. Once you are finished you can put all of it together. Now is the time to assimilate and determine what it is you've remotely viewed. Using all of your clues, can you now discover where the target is? Does it make sense to you? Can you go and look to see if you've accurately deciphered the data? Sometimes, alas, you may discover your object is gone for good. Hopefully that is not the case for you!

What Is Mediumship?

Mediumship is a gift that is used in conjunction with other psychic abilities. It is the receiving of interdimensional vibrations sent from Spirit to be translated into human concepts. Mediumship means exactly what the word implies, the go-between. Though when talking about connecting to the other side it carries the extra bonus of being metaphysical: being the medium or the channel between those alive and those who've passed on. The medium is psychic, though all psychics are not mediums. "To communicate with a spirit, a medium must raise his or her frequency and vibrational energy as a spirit lowers his or hers in order for both parties to obtain a frequency and vibrational energy match," shares Mark Anthony, who is a professional psychic, lawyer, and author of *Evidence of Eternity: Communicating with Spirits for Proof of the Afterlife*.

Mediums are able to communicate messages much in the same way we have conversations with our friends, though the information that comes through is usually not as clear. Using symbolism and references we are familiar with, the communicator tries to get us the messages as easily as possible so we can understand what they are trying to tell us. Every medium works differently but there are similarities throughout. When I do a reading and deceased loved ones come through, I usually hear their initial(s). Sometimes I will hear a name, which may just represent the initial, or I will get their actual name. Though this is with my clairaudience, I use all of my senses to receive the messages. As a medium, you are tasked with the job of proving the afterlife is real, and like a radio station, we can tune in to it.

Love lives on. It sounds cliché, but it really is true. When I conduct mediumship sessions, I can feel the love coming through from the other side. I know when there was a great connection here on earth and can tell when they are still expressing that emotion from the other side. I feel their energy with my clairsentient abilities. And I know when they are trying to reach out to hug someone. This happened during my reading with Tracy.

We were covering a lot of ground very quickly. Tracy's phone session was to last an hour and we had gone about halfway when her mom spoke up to let her know she was there, along with a bunch of others.

"Who is the 'L' name? Actually, there is someone who is kind of named after someone else?" I asked her.

"Wow. That would be my mom," Tracy replied, and I couldn't tell whether that was a good thing or not.

"Okay, great. There's another 'L'. Is she named for someone? 'Lo' name?" I continued.

"Well, she was Lois, and oh my, yes! Her dad was Louie!" she answered.

"I feel she is reaching her arms out to you. She is supporting you from the other side and sending her love to you. I feel like her arms are reaching to hug you," I told her, sure that her mom was definitely showing her affection from beyond.

"Oh," was all she said initially.

We went on with the reading—a bunch of other people coming through to let her know they were with her and saw what she was doing.

"I just have to ask, who had the chest issues? I also get something about cancer," I told her.

"That would be both my mom and my dad," she replied.

"Oh, good. Because I'm seeing your mother reaching out her arms to hug you still," I told her, convinced her mom was showing up to send her love from the other side as she had in life, though I still wasn't positive Tracy felt the same way.

"Oh, I'm so glad. My mom and I were so close. She was my everything. And she was definitely a big hugger. That makes so much sense," she said, and I could feel her tearing up on the other end of the phone.

I knew, because I felt the love, that she had had a good relationship. It was just one of those times that the emotions were overwhelming my client and she wasn't able to validate it immediately. I continued with the reading after that, bringing through messages using all of my psychic senses for Tracy as well as her family. They, the loved ones on the other side, were reaching out and sharing their messages any way they could, knowing that the more they sent the easier it would be to understand. They were right, as they always are.

You can practice mediumship by simply trying to tune in and gather evidence of the person that you are connecting to. Basically, it's no different than learning to use your psychic gifts, except that you connect to a specific person for yourself or someone else. You can develop your mediumistic abilities through practice, but having a natural gift always helps.

You may be a natural medium if:

- You talk to dead people.

- You see ghosts or other supernatural imagery.

- You hear messages from your deceased loved ones.

- You feel energy around you in areas where someone has died.

- You know that someone has or is about to pass before anyone else knows because they have visited you.

- You dream of your deceased loved ones or others vividly and you remember the dreams clearly.

• EXERCISE 20 •

Meet Your Deceased Loved Ones

The best way to develop your mediumistic skills is to practice using them. Go somewhere that is comfortable for you and where you won't be disturbed. You don't want to be interrupted while you are trying to connect to the other side. Bring your journal and your pen so you can write down any details, which will help you remember your experience after your session with the other side.

As usual, take a deep breath and close your eyes. Imagine yourself at the edge of a beautiful meadow filled with green grass and wild flowers. Take a step into the meadow and notice the lushness of the grass as your bare feet touch down. Like a blanket, the grass is soft and welcoming. You feel each pliable blade as it gently bends under your weight, holding you, protecting you. With each stride, you smell the fragrant blossoms dotting the meadow. You can see the bright colors of each of the flowers. Every hue of the rainbow is represented with the red roses, the orange lilies, the yellow daffodils, the green clovers, the blue hydrangea, the indigo coneflowers, the purple iris, and the white gerbera daisies. There are tulips in every color and flowering plants and shrubs as well.

As you continue walking through the meadow, every step brings a new lovely scent. Each pace allows you to see brilliant colors, colors that you've never even seen before. You can hear the honeybees as they pollinate, moving from bloom to bloom. Even the ants, as they work within their colonies, produce a hum as they move minute specs of dirt.

Off in the distance you notice a beautiful white tent, like a cabana. Its entrance of flowing sheets is gently blowing in a nice warm breeze, beckoning to you. As the tent billows, it sounds like a whisper calling you to come inside. You continue your way through the meadow toward the tent—hearing, seeing, feeling, and smelling everything around you.

As you reach the entrance to the bright white tent, the sun shines warmly down on you, and you can hear murmurs inside. Parting the sheets, you move into the tent and you observe light shadows moving slowly. You notice a plush, upholstered, round, silver bench in the center. You instinctively know it's a positive space for you to sit and you do so feeling totally at home, and perfectly protected.

Moving in front of you now, one of the shadows begins taking shape. It is one of your loved ones from the other side. You may pick up a scent specific to them or feel their love reaching toward you. You might be able to make out what they are wearing, what their hair looks like. Pay close attention now to what they have to tell you. Make a note of who it is, and if you have any questions for them, go ahead and ask them now. Let them stay as long as they want and listen to their messages. When they begin to fade, invite the next light shadow to join you and go through the same procedure. Invite all of your loved ones on the other side to join you.

After you've met everyone in the tent, just relax for a couple minutes and enjoy the positive energy. When you are ready, get up and walk out of the tent, leaving any negativity there to be recycled into positive energy. Walk back into the meadow and lay on the grass, reveling in the communications you just had with your deceased loved ones.

Open your eyes when you are prepared to come back, and write down everyone you met in your tent and everything they told you. Review everything you've recorded and say thank you to your loved ones. They worked very hard to come through to you.

Better with Practice

The more you work with your psychic gifts, the more you will develop them. Using practical psychic applications, such as remote viewing, mediumship, and telepathy, will allow you to increase your abilities even further. Enjoy the process and don't feel frustrated if you aren't able to tap in and perform these different practices right away!

TIPS

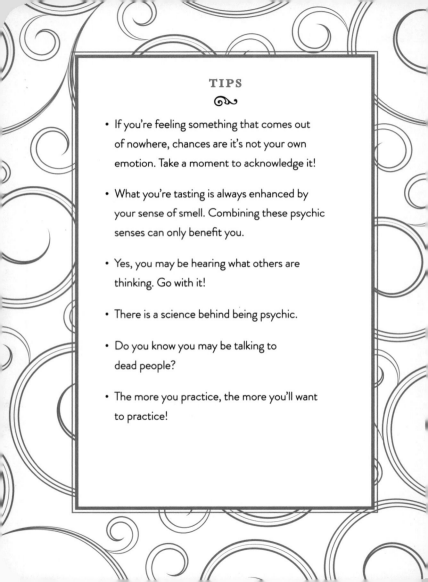

- If you're feeling something that comes out of nowhere, chances are it's not your own emotion. Take a moment to acknowledge it!

- What you're tasting is always enhanced by your sense of smell. Combining these psychic senses can only benefit you.

- Yes, you may be hearing what others are thinking. Go with it!

- There is a science behind being psychic.

- Do you know you may be talking to dead people?

- The more you practice, the more you'll want to practice!

Chapter Five

PSYCHIC TOOLS

Learning how to tap into your psychic abilities without the aid of anything else gives you a solid platform to jump from. Now you can begin taking advantage of the other resources available to you: psychic tools.

Why Do We Need Tools?

We use hammers and screwdrivers to make building and assembling easier. We use sewing machines and thread to stitch fabric. And we use computers to write and, yes, compute. We utilize tools to make our tasks easier. So, why not use tools to enhance your psychic abilities? Some people utilize psychic tools to help them connect to the energy of the person they are trying to read. At times it can be difficult to be sure of the messages we are receiving, especially if it's personal. Tools also offer more of an unbiased, nonjudgmental answer to questions we are trying to intuit for ourselves.

We often discount the messages we receive, thinking they are our imaginations speaking to us or that we are making it up. This is especially common when we are working hard to develop our psychic gifts. Using psychic tools allows us to impartially take in the information because it's more palpable. The messages are not just in our minds; they are something outside of us, which can make them easier to believe.

Better With or Without

Tools will not make you more psychic. So if you are depending on some object to turn you into the next Long Island Medium, chances are it's not going to happen. But if you are looking to understand the messages you are receiving, tools of the trade can definitely come to your aid. Utilizing these psychic instruments can be fun and you may very well feel a connection to one or even a couple of them. But, the reality is even though anyone can memorize a static meaning for each tarot card, that won't necessarily give them the ability to provide anyone with an in-depth intuitive reading. Using the tarot cards as a kind of home base and allowing your intuition to tune in to provide a more personal psychic reading will always trump the sterile memorized session. That said, however, using tools is a preference. It can allow you to have something tangible to start with, as most psychic information comes in more of an intangible form.

Just What Are Psychic Tools?

A good psychic tool is one that will help you translate complicated messages from the other side into human concepts we can understand. I bet you wouldn't imagine using dirt for divination, but what about rocks or cards or tea leaves? These are all common tools used in psychic readings. Rocks, stones, and crystals are used as is, or with symbols on them, also known as runes. There are all types of oracle cards. From regular playing cards to my deck of Psychic Symbols Oracle Cards to angel cards, there are thousands to choose from. Pendulums, too, are a normal tool and can run the gamut from a needle on a string to a fancy crystal wrapped in silver, crusted in jewels, and on a chain. If you can think of it, it can probably be used as a divination tool to aid your intuitive gifts.

Cards

Anyone can learn to read cards. Having said that, not everyone will be as adept at card reading as someone who has studied the practice for years. But you can learn to identify what the different colors, images, numbers, and words mean according to the card instructions as well as intuiting what they mean specifically to you. A good reader will always add their own interpreted message. Tarot can actually help you to develop your psychic abilities, according to tarot author Deborah Lipp. You can allow tarot itself to help you.

On my last birthday—yes, I just turned 21 again, for the 25th time—my friends and I went to a local restaurant/bar. While there I met someone who regularly frequented the bar every week to offer quick tarot card readings. When I saw him I thought, "I have to do this!" Most of the people there knew what I did for a living; in fact, most of them had had readings with me. When they saw this guy approaching me with the offer of a reading, they all looked at me and giggled, wondering what I was doing. But I, just like so many others, am always looking for a good reading.

"So you are doing tarot readings?" I asked him.

"Yes! Would you like one?" he replied.

"Sure," I said. He asked me what type of reading I wanted.

With tarot cards there are a few basic card spreads you can do, though the sky is the limit as to what you can develop. There is the past, present, future, where you lay one card out for each. Then there is the situation, the obstacles and advice, and best possible outcome. And, in my opinion, one of the best overall spreads, the Celtic Cross. This uses ten cards and covers all aspects of your life. So, this is the spread I wanted.

He laid out the cards and began reading them. I noticed immediately that he knew the cards by heart as he explained what each meant. I let him go through the whole thing, and then he asked if I had any questions. I asked him about a specific card. His answer matched word for word what he had previously said about it. So I asked him again to explain it in a different way. He said, "Okay," but then did exactly the same thing.

"You know, you are very knowledgeable in what the cards represent and what they mean, but I'd rather hear your intuitive interpretation now," I explained.

"Oh, okay," and he literally repeated it unchanged from how he had already delivered it.

Everyone was watching at this point and I felt like I was being deceitful, so I explained what I did for a living. I told him I thought he was really good at the memorized meanings of the cards but that he should maybe work on his psychic interpretations so he could add more depth to his readings. He obviously knew what he was doing with the cards, but he had yet to tap in to his psychic self. I hope one day he will develop his psychic abilities the way you are!

Like I said earlier, everyone can memorize what the cards mean, but discovering what they are about by using your intuition makes for a more in-depth interpretation. It also helps take you from deck to deck, utilizing the generic understanding of each individual card but also allowing for your personal intuitive spin to help decode the different cards in each type of deck. Often I use my own working deck of Psychic Symbols Oracle Cards that I have created. Each card has a symbol on it, along with a description. As with most symbols, there are universal descriptions, but there are always personal connections we make with certain symbols. Having your own intuitive translations from each deck helps to give your own perspective no matter what cards you are using.

It is about the interaction with the cards, not the actual cards, that helps you to develop your psychic abilities. After all, we've all done the cramming for a test, but did we actually gain knowledge, or did we just memorize it? Learning the generic meanings and allowing your intuition to open up is the best way to comprehend what you are reading in your deck spread. Tarot can give you unending knowledge; you need to take advantage of that and milk those cards for all they are worth!

Crystals and Rocks

Just as there are a huge variety of crystals and rocks that can be utilized, there are numerous ways to use them as psychic tools. All crystals can work with you and enhance your energy. You can work with a collection of crystals like quartz, rose quartz, or amethyst or other stones like calcite, aventurine, or azurite. All crystals can help you balance your body, mind, and spirit, and all are metaphysical tools. Although you can use certain stones for specific things, all of them aid in your energy readings.

There are stones you can use to help balance and open each one of your chakras and there are some that will enhance and attract or remove and clear particular traits, qualities, or tangible things. One of the easiest ways to determine which crystals work with each chakra is to match up the colors. Though it doesn't always correlate, more often than not a red tourmaline will help your first or root chakra and a blue lapis lazuli will aid your throat chakra (see chapter 2: Energy, Meditation, and Symbols; Chakras). By placing these stones on the actual chakras, it can help to kind of charge the energy of the chakra and balance it, which helps your mind, body, spirit connection.

Just like reading a crystal ball, crystals can be used for divination. A great way to use crystals to help develop your psychic abilities is to use the crystal as a scrying surface; something you look into to foretell the future or to view images about the present. Author and psychic Alexander Chauran explains how symbolic images that can be seen are believed to have meaning and purpose. Using a quartz crystal, for instance, one can see many things. By gazing into it, you may see actual shapes that have significance in some way. Or you may receive images from within that stir up psychic impressions. I like to use crystals to tell a story. As I look into a crystal's depths, I begin turning it. With each turn, each facet changes the shadows and shapes within, offering additional images. These images and shapes allow me to tell a psychic tale.

I did a reading for Chance, a teenager, a few years ago. He asked about crystals and how they worked. I told him I used them to describe an unfolding story and asked him if he had a specific question he wanted an answer to. He asked about lacrosse, and whether he should continue playing.

I chose a rose quartz because I had a large chunk of it and it just felt right. As I began looking into it, I saw stairs. The stairs could have been literal or symbolic, so I decided to keep looking. I then saw what looked like a ribbon. I decided I would share my interpretation with Chance at that point.

"I'm seeing stairs, which to me is symbolic of working your way up or steadily rising. So if we are talking about lacrosse, I don't see you as a shooting star, but I see you getting better—consistently better—and doing well. I also saw a ribbon. Again, I think it is symbolic of you achieving accolades or deserving awards for your playing. This, combined with the stairs, tells me you are on your way to making a name for yourself," I told him.

"That's cool!" he responded.

With just those two images I saw in the rose quartz I was able to help him understand he would do well to stick with lacrosse. But I knew I wanted to get some more for him so I turned the crystal again.

"Okay, this time I'm seeing what looks like a large building with a courtyard. It looks old and classic. I believe I am looking at a college, which indicates to me you will, indeed, play in college," I shared. "I also see what looks like a mask or what I think is probably a lacrosse helmet. This kind of confirms it for me!"

I then saw another image—something I hadn't ever seen before. I had to look a few times to make sure I was really seeing the image I thought I was seeing. I turned it a bit and was able to confirm what I saw.

"Now, this is really cute! I am seeing what looks like two stick figures, one with longer hair, holding hands and holding lacrosse sticks! I think I'm actually looking at you and a new girlfriend who also plays lacrosse!"

That did it for him. He was convinced. Chance decided he was going to continue playing the sport he loved. Although he had doubted he was good enough, he now believed it was possible to play and to play well enough to be on a college team. Well, that and the fact that he seemed to be in a happy relationship with a mutual laxer!

The best way to use crystals or stones to develop your psychic ability is to just do it. In the beginning, you may question what you are seeing in the stone. That is normal and perfectly acceptable. But after a while you will begin trusting the images you receive and even the energy you feel as you hold the crystals. Your scrying will help you view what is there, but your intuition will be the key to really interpret the messages. Using a clear quartz crystal is a great place to start because the easiest crystals to read will be ones that you can see into. You can also use stones that have a variety of colors, shapes, and images on the outside.

• EXERCISE 21 •
Scrying

Using a quartz crystal, or whatever crystal or rock you can get your hands on, you will do a reading. Just as I did, you can view your images in a kind of story format. I will provide the questions to prompt your answers and you can write both down in your journal. Like before, be sure to go somewhere comfortable and do a quick breathing exercise to ground yourself before you begin. When you are ready, pick up your crystal and clear your mind. Hold it in your hands so you can connect to its energy. Then answer the following questions by using the images you see as well as the energy you feel:

- What do you feel while holding the crystal?
- What is the first image you see?
- What does the crystal have to tell you?
- Should you continue on the same path you are currently on?
- What image(s) do you see when you ask about relationships?
- What image(s) do you see when you ask about finances?
- What image(s) do you see when you ask about a career?
- What image(s) do you see when you ask about family?
- What image(s) do you see when you ask about health?

Ask any other questions you may have of the crystal when you are done. Then go ahead and write down all of your answers in your journal. Did you see images? Did you feel answers? Did you get something for every question? Do the images resonate? Did they make sense? Did you expect the answers you received or were you surprised by them?

How did it feel, overall, to use crystals to enhance your psychic abilities? Was it comfortable or natural? Or did it feel awkward? Did it feel as though you had to work too hard to get your answers?

ჲ

Once you've begun using quartz you will find that using other rocks or crystals will come easier. Remember, what you see in the stones enhances your psychic abilities. Learn to trust what you see; even if what you are seeing initially appears as just lines in the rocks, the images will sort themselves out.

Pendulums

Pendulums use your energy to answer questions. A pendulum is an object on the end of a string or chain that can be used to answer yes or no questions. This is known as dowsing. Because of this, the sky is the limit as to what you can divine. The author of *Pendulum Magic for Beginners*, Richard Webster, writes that "learning to trust your first impression is a very important part of the process." Using a pendulum allows you to tune in to your subconscious, which in turn is connected to our psychic sense and the energy of the universe.

Pendulums can be made of crystals or wood or even plastic. Usually in a round or spherical shape coming to a point at the bottom, pendulums used for dowsing should be easily manageable and weigh only a few ounces. There is no right or wrong pendulum, as long as it is an object on the end of some type of cord. My first pendulum, which I still have and love, was a lead fishing lure on the end of a string. There really is no limit to the type of pendulum you can own, but there is a way to test them to see if they are right for you.

Using your clairsentience, or your clear feeling, you can determine if the pendulum you are interested in will work well with your energy. Testing it will allow you to make sure you have one that will enhance rather than take away from your psychic gifts. Using the following exercise, you can feel the differences between pendulums. You can either go to a store that sells pendulums or use a necklace or make a couple of pendulums using anything from a paper clip on a string to a sewing needle on a thread, etc. The point is to have a couple different types to choose from. Based on the weights of the pendulums they might move differently, but you should still get some action from them!

• **EXERCISE 22** •
Move It

Get your pendulums together. If you are at a store, choose as many as you want to try. Then decide on which you will start with first. Simply pick it up and hold it for a moment. If you feel energy, or even a charge coming from it, or it gets warm in your hand, that is the first indication that it may be a good match for you. Next, try doing a simple task with it and see if the energy flows through.

Holding it in your nondominant hand, wrap the cord over your ring finger and middle finger and let it hang. Anchor your elbow on a table or other inanimate object to prevent moving the pendulum accidentally. Then ask it to show you "Yes." Pay attention to how it moves. It should either move back and forth or around in a circle. Once you've determined which motion represents "Yes," ask it to show you "No." It should do the opposite. If it moved in a circle for "Yes," then you should see it swing in a straight line. If you get neither action for "yes" or "no," that is an indication that this pendulum may not be a good partner for you. If you received strong motions, it suggests a good energetic translator for you and should be considered a good tool.

Once you've finished with the first pendulum, continue testing the rest. Feel which responds best for you and which feels the most comfortable. You may find a few work well, and if that's the case, you can choose one or all! There's no reason to limit yourself to just one. Depending upon the situation you are dowsing for, you may choose one over the other to help clarify your psychic impressions.

Next, ask the pendulum that you prefer a simple question to determine if you're energy is indeed connected. Think of a question you already know the answer to. For example, "Am I male?" This should provide you with a definitive and correct response. If you don't get the right answer, it may mean you need to try a different pendulum or that you need to work on clearing your mind a bit more before asking another question. Remember, it is your subconscious that is connected to your intuition, and in turn the universe, providing the energy to move the pendulum. The only reason you would get a wrong answer is if you are blocking the energy by putting your conscious mind into it. Try the other pendulums out and see how they respond. Let go of expectations and just let it happen.

Did one work better than the others? Did you get answers? Did you like the process? Did it help you feel more intuitive? Were you surprised by any of it?

⚬⚬⚬

Above all, have fun using pendulums. It should be an enjoyable experience that helps encourage your psychic abilities to expand. There is an unlimited supply of pendulum combinations, so don't become discouraged if you don't have an easy go of it the first time. You can always try again!

It's Your Choice

As with most things psychic, it's your choice if you want to use tools or not. Some people find it to be easier to practice tuning in with tools while others find they get in the way of honing your psychic gifts. Either way, there is no reason you can't change your mind down the road.

There are many other divination tools available as well. Reading tea leaves or coffee grinds used to be very common and is still utilized by many who've learned this ancient technique of divining the swirls left in a person's tea cup. There's also palmistry. Palmistry is based on the principle that every palm is unique and contains our paths through life on lines, paths that include our careers, health, heart, finances, and more. They provide us with predestined events or predispositions to specific talents or gifts. Mine, for example, has many psychic stars and a writer's fork.

There are many good books to help you learn all about these different methods. Astrology uses the birth date, time of birth, and location of birth to acquire information about a person or their potential. Astrologers are also able to predict upcoming events by looking at your astrological birth chart. As you can see, the availability of psychic tools runs the gamut, and you need not empty your wallet to indulge in them. You need only the desire to try them out and learn about them.

TIPS
༄

- There are tools of the trade in every profession, why not with your psychic gifts?

- Interacting with the cards will allow your intuition to open up even more, like receiving a prompt to help you begin!

- There is no wrong way to read crystals.

- Just about anything can be used as a pendulum—what are you waiting for?

- Tools will always be there for you. You can utilize them when you want to!

TAKE-AWAY

As with most things psychic,
it's your choice if you want
to use the tools or not.
If it feels right, do it!

Chapter Six

OTHER WAYS TO CONNECT

As you've discovered, you can use tools to connect to the other side and to receive messages using your own energy. We are all meant to be intuitive. Learning how to utilize our psychic gifts is easier than we may ever have imagined. As a matter of fact, there are even more methods to be employed to help you decode and interpret.

Psychometry

Psychometry is not really a psychic sense but a method of reading. Psychometry is based on the principle that all objects hold energy and all energy can be read. By holding an object in your hand, you can use your clairsentience to feel the energy of the owner or the energy that is connected to the owner. For example, if the object is from someone who has passed, it may help you connect to that person. The object can also help provide you with information about the deceased.

Metal objects tend to hold energy the best. That's why jewelry works well when doing psychometry. Pictures also carry a lot of memories and energy. Some cultures believe pictures capture a person's soul. In order to receive messages from a picture, one needn't even look at it—just hold it. So, perhaps the photo does catch a bit of a person's soul. (Everything is energy, so it is plausible to think it possible, not to say you lose a bit of yourself in return, but it's kind of like leaving your fingerprint.)

Opening the Door While Dreaming: Is It Just a Dream?

Have you ever woken up wondering, "Was that just a dream? Or was it something more?" We've all had those dreams and even nightmares where we remember every single detail and it didn't actually feel like we were sleeping. When we woke it essentially felt like it was real, that it wasn't just a dream. There are many times we experience these types of dreams, but we write them off thinking they were merely manifestations of the huge ice cream sundae we ate at 10 p.m. the night before, or that it is simply our imagination at work. However, when what we experience at night is vivid, even technicolored, chances are we have experienced some type of psychic connection.

People come to me for a variety of reasons. They want readings mostly, but they also need validation about things that are happening in their lives—things like dreams they have had where it felt like more than just a dream. Often these involve deceased loved ones. Now, normally I am the medium in the session, but sometimes these dreams are indeed visitations from the other side and the client had no need for a medium to connect with them. When we are dreaming, we are not conscious of what's happening around us. This doesn't mean we can't snap to attention if we hear our child cry out or smell a fire brewing. What it does mean is we have gotten out of our way enough for our messengers from the other side to be able to communicate with us.

They want to use this opportunity. One client, Janice, explained how her mother had visited her in her dream before Thanksgiving. It was the first major holiday without her mother and also the first time she was going to cook and host the meal. She was nervous that she wouldn't be able to pull off the turkey and the stuffing. Janice dreamt about her mom, who proceeded to tell her in the dream exactly what ingredients to use in the stuffing and how to get it just right before stuffing the twenty-pounder that she would cook for a specific time at a certain temperature. When she woke up, she wrote everything down. She figured even if it was just a dream it still sounded good. And better yet, if it was her mom, it would be perfect. I shared with her that I felt it was indeed her mom and she should follow her instructions. Her meal turned out even better than her mom's used to be, and everyone remarked on the similarities and how good the turkey was!

Lisa came in and told me about a dream she had as a child that stayed with her all her adult years. She dreamt of her great-nonni, her great-grandmother, who came to her in their back stairway, which led up to where she had lived and spent her final days. Lisa's great-nonni told her she should get the lucky rabbit's feet out of the attic. When Lisa woke the next day, she told her mom all about the dream. Her mother pooh-poohed it because she was kind of freaked out at the suggestion. Her father said there were no rabbit's feet in the attic and never had been—he would know; he had grown up in the house.

Later in the day, Lisa and a bunch of her cousins were outside playing with the rest of the family. Lisa's mom shared with the other adults what Lisa had dreamt and they all concluded they had never seen any rabbit's feet, ever. As day turned to dusk, they looked up and saw a light on in the attic window. Having no reason for it to be on, since they had been home all day, and no one had gone into the attic, they all looked at each other perplexed. They went up into the attic and found, nailed around the window, six separate rabbit's feet. Lisa's parents were shocked to say the least. Sounds to me like Great-Nonni wanted to spread some luck around!

Another type of psychic dream is a prophetic dream. Prophetic dreams are ones that predict or tell of an upcoming event. It can be something good or something bad, it can be very brief with few elements, or it can be a long dream that plays out like an actual movie, complete with specific details. Either type will feel like something other than a regular dream during REM sleep. Instead, it will leave you wondering when you wake if it was really happening. It's that real feeling that separates it from the normal dreams, even though you usually won't be able to validate that it's real until possibly months later. This happened with me many years ago when I dreamt of a man with no leg. In my dream I saw a man in a marine uniform. I saw him somewhere in a desert on active duty, though I couldn't tell where and I couldn't make out his face. What I did see was two legs exactly where they were supposed to be. But right before I woke, I noticed one was missing, and I saw a symbol that is used in Reiki to help bring healing. (Reiki is a healing system in which the practitioner channels healing energy known as Universal Life Energy or Chi through to wherever the person needs it.)

I didn't make a connection to anyone or anything after my dream for quite a while. A few weeks later I received an email from someone who told me he wanted to come in for a Reiki session. We booked an appointment and when he came in I had a flash of the dream. I wasn't sure why until he told me he had served in the Marines and had lost his leg. He was okay with everything, had a prosthetic and a great attitude, but was experiencing phantom pain in the area of his amputation and was hoping Reiki would help that.

Having prophetic dreams sometimes just gives you a heads up that something or someone is coming. It doesn't have to be a life-altering or life-changing event, just like all psychic communications are not life and death. But, there are some that can definitely make you think.

My mom, for instance, dreamt of a cruise chip sinking; no, it was not the *Titanic*! She saw a newspaper displaying a headline that the cruise ship went down. When she woke up she believed it to be just a dream. The next night she slept soundly. In the morning she saw her mother reading the newspaper. The headline described a cruise ship going down the day before. When she told her mother and father, they did not believe her dream had occurred. They just thought she must have heard about it somewhere, but she knew she had seen the headline in vivid detail while dreaming.

Dreams can also answer your questions. They can connect your psyche to the energy of the universe and provide you with direction. You can train your subconscious to reveal intuitive details to you while you sleep. This can prove useful when you have a hard time getting true psychic answers, especially if you doubt what you receive. It allows you to get out of your own way enough to let the information come through.

Often dreams present us with symbols. Our minds are able to process the symbols quickly and more easily at times, and our subconscious can relate to the imagery much like the way our messengers communicate with us. Robert A. Johnson, author of *Inner Work: Using Dreams and Active Imagination for Personal Growth,* explains that our dreams use a special language-symbolism.

• EXERCISE 23 •
In Your Dreams

Tonight before bed, decide on something you desire or need an answer to. Write it down. Is it something you want? Or something you want to accomplish? If so, write it down in question format, "How can I bring _____ into my life?" or "How can I make _____ happen?" or "What do I need to do to accomplish _____?" If it is something you want to know, write it like, "What is going to happen with _____?" Or "Is _____ going to happen?" or "How is _____ going to work out?"

Whatever you want to know, shape it in the form of a question. Once you have your question written out, say it aloud ten times. This is to put the energy out into the universe. Then say the words, "During my slumber please answer my question ..." and repeat the question again. Have your journal and a pen right next to your bed. Then put the question under your pillow and go to bed with the intention of receiving the answer to your question while you sleep.

After you wake up, write down everything you remember dreaming about immediately in your journal. Keep writing until you can recall nothing else. Then look at what you wrote. Does the answer to what you've asked immediately jump out at you? Did you dream with many details? Is there any imagery or symbolism? When you translate any symbolism, does that help to bring you answers? If you can't figure out exactly what you've dreamt right away, move the information around. Translate any symbolic images you dreamt. Then look at it again and see what it reveals.

If you don't believe you received the answers, you need go through the same ritual again the following night. Continue doing it for seven days. By the end of the week you will find many different dreams may have overlapping information. Review everything your subconscious has shared with you and you will discover your answers.

Dreams can be both fascinating and mysterious, and if you take the time to decode them, they can offer you insight as well as a way to connect to your deceased loved ones. Every dream will not be a psychic event, so decipher them with an open mind. Dreams can take us to places we might never go in our waking state, and they can provide us with fodder and inspiration to create a better life. And, they can also help us develop our intuitive abilities and bolster our connection to the other side.

Synchronicity

How many times have you said, "Wow! What a coincidence!" Well, guess what? Those situations may be more than mere coincidence. In the metaphysical world, these connected occurrences are known as synchronistic events. These synchronicities are not cause-and-effect happenings, they are more like seemingly random events. Once you realize they are connected, there is no denying there is some type of deeper meaning—you're acknowledging them for a reason. They are significant. When these little or big coincidences happen, they make you pause and wonder for a minute, until, if you're lucky, that aha moment kicks in and you understand just a little bit more of why you are present in the universe.

Carl Jung originally coined the term "synchronicity" in an essay he wrote in 1955 to define an acausal connecting principle, which is also the name of his paper. Everything and everyone is linked together. Thoughts, actions, emotions, and beliefs all create energy. This is why synchronicities occur—because the energy is connected. Once something is put out into the universe, it creates a ripple effect, like the butterfly that flaps its wings. A naturally occurring cycle of synchronistic events can be expected when you are developing your intuition. The more you become aware they are happening, the more in tune you feel with the universe and the less surprised you are when the next one arises in your life.

I like to think of myself as an average, normal person. I am not famous or rich by any means. I have published books and I do readings worldwide, but I would never consider myself renowned or even prominent in the world I live in. After all, don't famous people have house-cleaners and childcare providers and fabulous shoes? So when something happened to me and my friends, it was a total shocker, but I realized afterward that it was definitely a synchronistic event.

I was out to dinner with my husband and a couple of friends at a local steak restaurant. We were all having a great time; it was the perfect mix of food, flowing drinks, and great conversation. During dinner one of my friends asked how my book was coming. (I was writing my third at the time, *Psychic Abilities for Beginners*.) I told them it was going well, but as usual I was running right up to my publishing deadline. They exclaimed, and my husband joined in, that I was famous—to which I rebelled. I was not famous, but I sure was enjoying what I was doing!

"Really? You are known worldwide! Your books are sold all over! And you do readings for people everywhere and are constantly on radio shows!" they continued, convinced that they were sitting with someone who, even though I was normal to them, would be known to others as something pretty special.

Again, I denied it. "If I were famous I would be paying for your dinners!" I joked. "And people would recognize me!"

We finished up dinner and decided to move our party to an entirely different area of the restaurant. There was a barroom on the other side of the building, about four rooms away. We decided to go and have a couple of after-dinner drinks.

We sat down at the bar and ordered. After we finished our first round, we decided we would take the party somewhere else; we were getting ready to leave when a group of women approached us.

"Oh, my! Wow! Are you *the* Melanie Barnum?" they asked all at once.

"Huh?" was my very intelligent, author-like response.

I looked over to see my husband's chest puffing and my friends staring. My husband, Tom, was extremely proud and my friends, along with myself, were somewhat shocked. I was still wondering if I was in trouble for something, to be honest!

"Yes, yes she is!" Tom exclaimed.

"Are you the Melanie Barnum that is the psychic and author?" they continued.

I was still racking my brain trying to figure out what was wrong. Granted, my brain did have a bit of alcohol floating in it at the moment, so I was a bit slow on the uptake.

"Yes?" I finally answered.

"Oh my God! I just finished your first book! I loved it! I have heard so much about you!" they continued, as they all chimed in with professional accolades for me.

"Oh, I'm so glad you enjoyed it!" I responded, totally blown away.

This wasn't the first time something like this had happened, but it was pretty close. We chatted a bit more and then made our exit, with by now the whole bar staring at us, wondering just who the heck I was!

This was a synchronistic event. It was like the universe was slamming me. It was asking me to acknowledge that although I didn't feel famous, my work was undeniably reaching many people and affecting them in ways I couldn't imagine. I was humbled by their accolades and it made me feel like I was doing the work I was supposed to be doing.

I was extremely appreciative after that, and as a matter of fact, it has become a joke amongst my friends. When I'm introduced in a social setting they will say, "And do you know *the* Melanie Barnum?" with a giggle. I can say I am more than flattered every time!

The more in tune you are with your intuition, the more you'll notice synchronicities, and vice versa. Becoming aware is the only tool you need to recognize these destined coincidences. This, then, can begin another effortless layer of your psychic development. Working with your abilities can grow into an everyday custom that will enhance and attract an abundance of gifts. Sonia Choquette, celebrated spiritual teacher, visionary, and storyteller (and one of my favorite teachers), talks about how the two, synchronicity and intuition, can aid each other. In her book *Tune In: Let Your Intuition Guide You to Fulfillment and Flow,* she writes, "As you practice daily rituals to touch base with your inner voice, ... the more you'll experience the magic of intuition. Synchronicity replaces struggle."

• EXERCISE 24 •
Synchronize!

Ideally you would have a multitude of synchronistic events to use for this exercise, but realistically, they can be hard to remember. So, this exercise may take awhile to complete, and that is okay.

Open your journal to a fresh page. Write down any synchronistic events you can remember. For example, it could be as basic as having a thought in your mind and then someone walks by you and says the same exact thing you were just thinking. Now, this is the part that can take awhile. Record every coincidence you can recall. Remembering them is tricky, but hopefully you'll be able to pull a few up from your memory.

Once you've recorded the situations that you can, it's time to look at each one and analyze them a bit.

- What was going on when each occurred?

- What did you gain by recognizing them?

- What were you able to take away from the synchronicity, if anything?

- Were you shocked when it happened?

- Were you surprised?

- Were you happy or excited?

- Were you puzzled?

- Did you notice anything else of significance about each event? Write it down.

- Do you notice a pattern?

- Does it feel like you have to be meta-phorically hit over the head to grasp a concept that these synchronicities are trying to show you?

- Do you feel like they're connected?

- Were you unable to recall any synchronistic events?

Give Me a Sign

Signs are the little intuitive or synchronistic nudges you actually see externally. I've had quite a share of synchro-nistic signs myself. One such event happened today. I was in the grocery store and my elbows were hurting—probably because they have been bent for long periods of time since I've been writing so much. I had been debating all day long whether I should take ibuprofen or not. I tend to shy away from it because it actually makes me get hot and sweat easily, so I had been avoiding it. But as I was walking up the bread aisle, I began thinking about the pain I was in and wondering if I should just bite the bullet and take the medicine to help my joints feel better. Just as I was coming to the end of the aisle, there was an oversized display of ibuprofen—buy one get one free. I took that as a sign, a synchronicity that I should indeed take the pain reliever.

Synchronicities do not need to be major, huge, cloud opening, and lights shining down from the heavens events. They can be simple, ordinary occurrences that make you say hmmm. Some synchronistic signs are put in our path by the universe to answer our sometimes unasked questions. They are the ibuprofen display that was there exactly when I needed to see it. It's a synchronistic sign when you are trying to decide where to shop today and you turn on the television and there's a commercial for one of the stores you were thinking of now offering you the opportunity to come in today for a special deal!

The wow factor is there whether it is a big happening or something simple and seemingly insignificant.

Signs pop up when we least expect them. They guide us to where we need to be, usually at a time when they can significantly help us. But we can also ask for them. We've all heard ourselves or our friends say, "God, give me a sign!" when we need to make a decision or when we want to know everything will be alright. And we've prayed, in our own way, for something to show up that will clearly illuminate the route we need to take. These signs are put in our path to encourage us and there's no reason we can't ask for them to show up!

• EXERCISE 25 •
Just Ask

Think of something you'd like to receive guidance on. It could be a question about your career or a relationship. It can be about whether to go on a family vacation or just a trip with your friends. You can ask for a sign to help you decide if you're making the right decision regarding your kids or if the gym you are considering joining will help you reach your goals. All of these are valid questions. You can ask for a sign to show up in order to assist you with whatever you choose.

After you've settled on what your question or subject is, write it down in your journal. Then it's time to wait. Pay attention during your day. Your sign will show up. You may receive more than one, so continue being open throughout the entire day.

If, for some reason, you've missed your sign, try again tomorrow! When you notice the sign answering your question, write it down and answer these questions:

- Did it answer your question or give you direction?
- Did it validate what you were already thinking?
- Was it the answer you expected?
- Was it the sign you expected?
- Did you have to search for a sign or did it randomly show up?
- Does it feel right?
- Are you going to listen to it?

If, after you've reviewed everything you feel, you still need help or need more information or guidance, ask for another sign! You can always request more assistance from the other side. They are there for you—take advantage of it!

Remember, synchronicities are evident only when we realize they are happening. Case in point: as I was thinking I wanted a snack, my phone beeped. I had been tagged in a post on Facebook—it was a video showing how to make ice cream from bananas. Yum, sounded good, but that would take at least a couple of hours. Then, as I kept writing with the TV on in the background, I looked up and there was a chef peeling bananas to make banana bread. *Okay, I get it, but banana bread takes too long and I have a deadline to meet!* I thought.

I decided to take a quick break. As I walked into the kitchen my husband was there and he said, "You need to eat these bananas before they go bad." Duh, I shouldn't have to be hit over the head. I needed to have a banana!

We are so lucky to be able to enhance our psychic abilities simply by being open to what the universe provides. Intuition and synchronicity can sometimes feel like two separate phenomena. When we study psychic abilities, we know that we mostly intuit internally, whereas synchronicities and signs present themselves externally. They are more tangible, something you can actually see outside of your mind's eye. However, they play a huge roll in the energetic connection to the universe, which obviously allows your psychic gifts to expand exponentially!

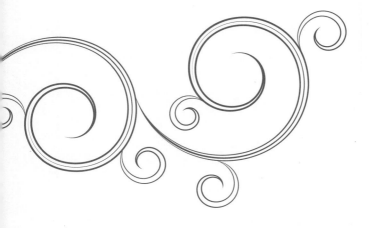

TIPS

∽

- Pay attention to your dreams. They carry a lot of pertinent information.

- Chances are, that coincidence is not merely a coincidence!

- Open your eyes so you can see the signs!

Chapter Seven

BRINGING IT INTO YOUR REALITY

Making the effort to align your mind, body, and spirit is important when you are developing your psychic abilities. Keeping yourself from overloading is a great way to fend off exhaustion. Staying grounded as much as possible is a necessity. Don't make it a last-ditch effort when you are feeling weak. Instead, make it a priority to ground your energy regularly.

We're All In It Together

We are all connected. Because of that we sometimes take on other people's energy without realizing it, especially if you're an empath (see chapter 4: Other Psychic Senses and Practices). What is not as widely understood is that if we take on someone else's energy, there is usually an exchange. When we begin to feel emotions that feel odd or that aren't ours, we may recognize that it's someone else's stuff. The problem, though, is we have also given away some of our energy in return. Sending their energy back, or kicking it out from yours, can leave you feeling weakened. You need to be sure to get yours back!

Psychic work in general can leave you feeling tired or drained. It takes a lot out of you when you are working so hard. When I have a long day of readings, I feel exhausted and hungry even though I protect myself before every session. I come home from my office and feel almost as though I'm walking in slow motion. I have to sit and ground myself for a while and meditate a bit to not only shed the energy I've taken on from communicating with the other side all day but also to recharge my own batteries. It can definitely leave me feeling a bit worn.

Cutting the Cord

Another way to help you balance when you are practicing so hard is to remove any energetic cords that are pulling at you. These are cords I liken to fiber optic lines stretching from you to everyone you know and everything you're involved in. Imagine when someone is mentally or emotionally tugging you. It's the same thing with energy. When using an infrared camera, you can often even see the energetic pull. When I see it in my mind's eye I envision the fiber optics cable lighting up bright green when it is a healthy connection to someone, and it gets darker, all the way to muddy red when someone is taking up too much of your energy. When you are communicating positively with someone I see it as bluish purple. Other cables just seem to drag you down. It's these cables or cords that you sometimes need to cut or release.

If you feel like someone or something is taking too much energy from you or making you tired, it's probably time to take matters into your own hands. There are many psychic vampires out there that can suck you dry if you don't detach from them. You've probably heard the phrase "cut the cord." It's exactly what we're talking about here. It's time to cut the cord—from you to the energetic drag. It's a simple thing to do and something you should continue to do on a regular basis to make sure you keep your own energy positive and healthy. Alternatively, you can also do this by sending positive energy back down the cord toward the other person instead of cutting loose the cord that connects you.

• EXERCISE 26 •
Cut the Cord

Sit and relax. Take a few deep breaths. Close your eyes and breathe again. Then, when you are ready, start thinking about where all of your energy is going. Visualize the people who are sucking the life out of you, sending negative energy, or needing way too much from you. Envision anyone who is constantly causing you grief—anyone that you can't seem to break from who is abusive in some way or uses you in some way. Envision the negative situation that you no longer need to be part of. Think of anyone that is causing drama that you no longer need to deal with. If it's someone you love, don't worry. We will handle that.

Now, visualize the first person that you feel total negativity from, and imagine there is a cluster of fiber optic cables traveling from them to you. Find it on them, then find it on you. Notice where they are attached. Are they going directly to any of your chakras? Once you've located it, see what color it is. If it's all negative energy, it is probably dark and murky.

Imagine you have some very sharp scissors. Now pick up the cord in your hand and cut the specific negative strand. You can feel each bit of the thick cable as it cuts apart. Cut the cord until there are no more damaging ties from that person or situation to you. If you want, you can send positive energy down the remaining strands to deter negativity from coming through instead of cutting them.

Keep cutting the cords or sending positive energy down them, one by one, until you get to a loved one or family member or friend that is causing you grief but who you don't want to cut free from entirely. Now, look at the elements of the cable going from that person to you. Remember, each cable is made of a multitude of little strands. Look at the strands individually. Is there a difference in color? As soon as you discover the details of the cable, you are able to separate the strands and use the scissors to cut only the negative parts to keep the positive aspects intact. Do this for all of the people or situations you want to keep positively in your life.

When you've finished, you should feel lighter and less weighted. You should no longer feel the pull of the psychic vampires sucking you dry. Instead, you should feel like you can conquer the world! Were you able to see the people? the situations? the colors? If not, no worries. You know how to cut the cords or send the positive energy now so you can repeat it as often as you need to.

You never want to lose who you are, so you always want to check in with yourself and see if anything is at risk. We all experience energy drains, whether it's from just doing the psychic work or from others extracting what they need from you without replenishing what they've taken. You've learned how to clear your energy, recharge your batteries, and realign your mind, body, and spirit. Doing this on a regular basis will enable you to continue developing your psychic abilities without wiping yourself out. You and your gifts are worth it.

What About Grace?

You have to trust yourself. You won't always be able to immediately validate everything you get or every psychic thought you share with others. Sometimes, actually most times, you just have to be patient. Everything works out the way it's supposed to. Cliché, I know, but frequently true.

Do you remember in the beginning of the book I told you about my friend, Grace? She was hoping to buy a house in Rhode Island. When she first asked me, I saw a small brown house, but then I saw a gray and white building. She sent me a picture of a brown house with a gray and white shed that she was putting an offer on to immediately validate what I told her. What she couldn't validate were the references to beans, the letter C, and an abundance of orangey balls.

A couple of weeks went by and I heard from Grace. She had put an offer in but was having problems with the property. She wanted to know if I could tell her anything else. I shared that I just saw the gray and white, now, and repeated the other information I had previously seen. She would also need to redo the flooring, and there was something funky up with the toilet, but neither would be major issues for her.

She then sent me a few pictures of a couple of other cottages she was considering. Immediately, there was a gray and white one that stood out. It was in a community on the water but within a block of the beach. On a dirt road, it had a gravel driveway.

"What is the address of this one?" I asked her, sensing this was it.

"It's 132 Succotash Road" she responded, excited.

"It feels right to me!" I told her.

I looked up the address online and told her this was it, but she had the address wrong. It was 132 C, which explained the C I had seen. I also saw a bunch of orangey balls on one side of the house—there was a large tomato garden and the tomatoes were just beginning to ripen. It was all making sense! Grace put an offer in and bought the house. She called me from Rhode Island to fill in the rest. The flooring she indeed had to replace.

"And, you're never going to believe this. I talked to the realtor. The community just finished updating the septic lines outside the house which is a great thing because the toilet was constantly backing up for the previous owners!" she exclaimed. "I just had to tell you how right you were!"

"Wow! That's so cool! And I'm glad you won't be living in sewage! But, what about the beans?" I asked her.

She laughed and said, "Maybe it was connected to the toilet reference?"

"Ha! I don't think so," I told her.

Then, I thought of the address. "Wait a minute! Succotash is made from lima beans! That's the bean reference!"

Done. She bought the house and you better believe I will be visiting her for sure! Even though I wasn't sure the house she was validating originally was what I was psychically getting, I went along with it because it seemed to fit well. But like I always tell my clients, everything will work out the way it is supposed to. That first run down brown house was not the house for her. This one, the cute little gray and white cottage, however, was just perfect!

Now What Can You Do With What You've Done?

Your perception of your reality should have shifted a bit by now. What you may have once thought a long shot is now a definite possibility. The boundaries of what you once believed have long since blurred and the knowledge you've gained is something you will never forget. The skills you've discovered or reignited are yours to keep and nourish into something even more incredible. It's now up to you to continue practicing. You deserve to enjoy your newfound or reinvigorated talents; they are gifts after all!

Now that you've begun you know there is no turning back. You can use your abilities in so many amazing ways. Whether you decide to use them on a personal level or take them out into the world to help others, there are a myriad of opportunities available for you. Many have discovered their true calling after they've tuned in to the energy of the universe and embraced their guides and loved ones from the other side. Have you thought about who you would be if you allowed yourself to reimagine *you*?

Obviously, doing readings for others is now a possibility. You need to be careful to only offer readings when you are ready. It is completely ethical to read people if you let them know you are practicing your newly developed gifts, but you want to be sure to present the disclaimer in order to be fair; at least until you are ready. Otherwise, people will be relying on the information you give them, thinking you are already a professional and they can trust that what you are getting is totally legit and valid. Which, in actuality, it can be. It's up to you to be sure you feel capable and confident and can bring evidence to the table about what you are bringing through. You don't just want to give people random information that can't be validated; you want to make sure you are getting some psychic hits. Remember, not everything will be validated immediately, but there is usually some information you bring through that can be.

• EXERCISE 27 •
Read On

It's time for some fun. Let's do a reading! Grab a friend who doesn't mind having a reading done, or grab one of their friends that you don't know who would love to let you try. Ask them to bring an object or two for you to read.

Sit across from each other with a piece of paper and a pen. Breathe deeply and close your eyes. Imagine you can feel roots reaching into the center of the earth from the bottoms of your feet. Allow the earth's energy to rise up and spread positive, grounding energy through all of your chakras, from your root chakra all the way up to your crown.

Breathe in this amazing energy, and when you are ready, ask your partner to place their object in your hand with your eyes still closed. Sit with the object. Allow the energy to transmit any symbols, thoughts, feelings, images, or sounds to you. Then, open your eyes and write down anything that came to mind. Remember, do not discount what you get. What may be insignificant to you could be extremely important to the sitter (the person you are reading for).

When you are done recording everything you've received, ask the object to answer the following questions:

- What colors come to mind?
- Is the owner of the object alive or dead?
- If dead, how did they die?
- Any initials, letters, or names?
- Any numbers?
- Any specific locations: states, cities, landmarks, buildings, etc.?
- Any foods?
- Vitamins they need?
- Any names from spirit trying to come through?
- Career for who object represents or the owner of the object?
- Any specific songs?
- Pets or animals connected to or coming through?
- Any other images?
- Any other sounds?
- Any other thoughts?

- Any other feelings?
- Any other tastes or smells?

Continue recording anything else that comes to mind and then share with your sitter everything you received. Were they able to validate any of it? Some of it? Most of it? Mone of it? If all of it made sense, awesome! You did great! If none of it made sense, again, awesome! You gave it your all! Continue practicing. You may find the more you do it the more relaxed you become and the better the reading is.

There's Still More

Having new psychic skills provides new perspectives. This means you see things three-dimensionally, rather than just one-dimensionally. You are able to provide alternatives based on your extrasensory perception. This will assist you in making smart choices and intuitive decisions, which are more informed than simply using your five physical senses. These perspectives can assist you with relationship questions and career options and more for yourself and others.

Imagine using your new gifts to medically heal people. Focusing your powers on research while following your gut instincts and your clairsentient feelings—combined with what may be an already enriched curiosity or ability in the health field—can jump us light-years ahead in finding cures for disease, illnesses, etc. Taking it to a different medical arena, it is more than conceivable that you can now tune in to an individual's aura and discover what is ailing them so you can assist in their healing process. Bringing it down to a personal level, you can help yourself and your loved ones feel better by adjusting yours or their energy. Yes, you can definitely create a path toward healing now that you've opened the doors.

Being part of the medical community is not your only way to use your psychic abilities to work on healing others. Collaborating with the other side, you can talk to the deceased loved ones of others to help those still here move on from loss. Grief when a loved one dies is a phenomenal thing. It can cause us to practically lose our mind with sadness. It is the combination of loss and anger that creates a painful cycle which makes it hard to work through or get beyond in any way. Knowing that our loved ones are still with us can help us experience that grief in a different way. Being the medium and sharing their love and messages from the other side to those in pain can bring you a sense of fulfillment and gratitude like no other.

You can use your intuition on a more personal level as well. Knowing who to get into business with can make or break you financially. Having an intuitive sense can keep you from blindly jumping into bed with just anyone. The same can be said for relationships. Whether an intimate relationship or just a friendship, being a good judge of character is easier when you use your intuition.

We've discussed a lot of human communication, but what about animal communication? Remember Max? The loving dog that was so excited to go to aqua therapy that he unfortunately leaped to his death when he jumped out of the car? He sent love from the other side to Nicole. Even though I am not primarily an animal intuitive, I have animals that come through all the time to say hello and send love to their humans here on Earth. I've had dogs, cats, guinea pigs, bunny rabbits, fish, and even rats say hi, but I think the best one was the pet snake. I couldn't figure it out at first, but I developed a lisp during the session—which made me a little crazy until they acknowledged losing a snake! He was coming through, making me talk with an *sssss* sound like a snake so my client would recognize him.

There are virtually no restrictions to what you can now do with your psychic abilities. The most important thing to remember is to always read with integrity. Don't ever twist what you receive to fit what your sitter wants to hear or make things up to spite them. And, finally, leave your ego at the door. Reading for yourself or others with your ego will never work. It will always come out wrong and even block you from receiving anything. Ego is fear based and fear is never a good place to start. Read from a place of love—that's why we are all here after all.

Give Yourself a Hand!

You've done a lot of work throughout this book. You've opened your eyes to what may be a new way of looking at life. Your approach to situations has now been altered. Your mind has forevermore discovered alternative reasons for things that happen. You are open. This is your time to enjoy your psychic abilities. You've got both feet planted in the present, in the here and now, and it's your perfect opportunity to use those feet to jump in and use everything you've learned to expand and enhance your bountiful gifts. Whether you decide to go back and practice the exercises again, or you bring your talents out to the world, you have already changed your life for the better. Take advantage of it!

TIPS

- You don't need to hold on to any negative energy.

- Be patient and trust what you get.

- You've got this.

- You can choose to do great things for yourself
  and others with your newly developed gifts!

Acknowledgments

The psychic world is growing by leaps and bounds. Every day there are more believers, more practitioners, and more teachers to help spread the word that there is more to this life than what we perceive with our five physical senses. It is to all of these people that I say thank you! You've opened your mind, body, and spirit and helped so many discover who they are and who they can be. You are helping pave the way to understanding.

A huge thank you as well to all of my clients, past and present, who have allowed me to be part of their awakening and welcomed me into their lives by letting me connect them to their deceased loved ones. Without you, what I do would mean nothing.

And, of course, another big shout-out to all of you who've let me share your stories with others so they too may learn how amazing our loved ones are in the afterlife!

All of my teachers, including my friends, family, and clients, deserve my gratitude as well. Whether you were aware you've assisted in my learning process or not you deserve a pat on the back. Not only are you helping me, you are helping so many others.

Tom, my husband, encourages me always, telling me I am so much better than I give myself credit for. My daughter, my Nugget, who looked at me today and randomly said, "Mom, you are so beautiful!" and my Little Bug, who tells me, her mama, that she is so proud of me! They echo what they learn and are filled with love, kindness, and intelligence, and I couldn't be prouder of the beautiful reflections I see looking back at me.

And, of course, my mom. I love her more than even I can imagine, and I miss her terribly. I just wish she would show up as a full-bodied spirit! I mean, really. I do see everyone else's dead people, I want to see her, too!

Thanks to my brilliant, beautiful sister, Tammy. She is one of my biggest cheerleaders, and I am one of hers. She deserves my total respect and has it for everything she does for me and others, as well as everything she is! And my brother, Adam, who, and I will swear by this, is smarter than us all and who should be writing his own version of the Great American Novel. Mom always said we all have one in us, and I believe it's his turn!

Bibliography

Anthony, Mark. *Evidence of Eternity: Communicating with Spirits for Proof of the Afterlife*. Woodbury, MN: Llewellyn Publications, 2015.

Bodine, Echo. *The Gift: Understand and Develop Your Psychic Abilities*. Novato, CA: New World Library, 2003.

Chauran, Alexandra. *Crystal Ball Reading for Beginners: Easy Divination & Interpretation*. Woodbury, MN: Llewellyn Publications, 2011.

Choquette, Sonia. *Tune In: Let Your Intuition Guide You to Fulfillment and Flow*. Carlsbad, CA: Hayhouse, 2013.

Dillard, Sherrie. *Develop Your Medical Intuition: Activate Your Natural Wisdom for Optimal Health and Well-Being*. Woodbury, MN: Llewellyn Publications, 2015.

Johnson, Robert A. *Inner Work: Using Dreams and Active Imagination for Personal Growth*. San Francisco, CA: Harper & Row, 1986.

Jung, Carl. *Synchronicity: An Acausal Connecting Principle*. Trans. R. F. C Hull. Hove, East Sussex: Routledge, 1991.

Kenner, Corrine. *Crystals for Beginners: A Guide to Collecting & Using Stones & Crystals*. Woodbury, MN: Llewellyn Publications, 2006.

Lipp, Deborah. *Tarot Interactions: Become More Intuitive, Psychic & Skilled at Reading Cards*. Woodbury, MN: Llewellyn Publications, 2015.

Webster, Richard. *Pendulum Magic for Beginners: Tap into Your Inner Wisdom*. St. Paul, MN: Llewellyn Publications, 2002.

Alex Cell 657-3355
Benny 206-471-5786
Mike 712-9001
Love 206 475-6521
True 206-468-6641
Rob 705-0486
Chris green lake 206-498-3387
Meg+Armond 425-902-8874
Kemy 206 566 4254
Raleh 206-251-3359
Raisell 206 880-4351
Dreadlock D 206 424-1024
713-2370